The Silent
Screaming

Raising a Child with Psychiatric Disorders
& Mental Health Challenges

Rhonda A. Thompson

Author, Speaker, Pediatric Nurse, Healthcare Executive

For more information, or quantity discounts, visit TheSilentScreaming.com

ISBN: 979-8-218-28181-6

Editing: Robin Steinweg • RobinSteinweg.com
Design: BookableMedia.com

WHAT THEY'RE SAYING

"Stories like Joshua's are so important to share, but rarely get told. Families typically deal with the behaviors of their kiddos behind closed doors, creating isolation for the entire family unit. Having open dialogue about our children who are struggling with psychiatric disorders lets others know it's ok to get help. This story also speaks to generational trauma and how transparency and treatment help to break the cycle for future generations. Although Joshua will have lifelong challenges, he has a fighting chance thanks to the love, support and advocacy supplied by Rhonda and her husband. It is a testimony to the difference just one adult can make in the life of a child."

Jessica Knudsen, LCSW, FACHE
CEO/President, Clarity Child Guidance Center

"This is an important story. It's not a story about shame, it's not a dirty little secret to be hidden from the world. It is about resilience and determination and most of all love, and it will speak to those who can relate in the most tragic of ways. Unfortunately, the story is not unique. But because of that, it can give power to others that need to know they are not alone."

Jodie Thompson
Attorney in Wyoming

"This book should be a must read for educators in every facet, for it is easy to label a child as "defiant," "unruly," "spoiled," "coddled" when the mere truth may just be that the child is fighting their way to find themselves in a world that did them very unjustly in their most formative years before the age of five and quite possibly continued beyond. While these children are often the most difficult in school, they are the ones with the greatest needs, especially for patience, kindness, time, and love. This author sheds light on how abuse affects so many in such different and traumatic ways."

Sherry Bailey
Educator, Teacher

FINDING THE RIGHT THERAPIST FOR YOUR FAMILY

*Access your free gift
from Rhonda*

Thank you for your support and purchase of this book.
Please feel free to access this free video training
on finding the right therapist for your family.

TheSilentScreaming.com/gift

Dedicated to Joshua

You are loved, you are seen, you are heard, and you are important.

You will always be my Boober. Love, Mom

CONTENTS

FOREWORD

The Silent Screaming offers an intimate look into familial child abuse and the terrible developmental consequences and psychological scars that an abused child can experience—often permanently. Ms. Thompson describes her nephew Joshua's childhood abuse with compassion, empathy, and sometimes the raw frustration that accompanies raising a child with developmental, cognitive, and psychological disorders. The storyline that *both* Ms. Thompson and her nephew were abused by family members underscores the unfortunate and heartbreaking reality of multigenerational child abuse.

A poignant, honest storyline reveals the commitment Rhonda and her husband employed in raising Joshua to reach his potential. Ms. Thompson descriptively shares both good and bad in her struggle to deal with and manage her nephew's cognitive disabilities and his mental health challenges with unconditional devotion. Ms. Thompson also faced the judgment and unkind words of other parents who had no understanding of Joshua's challenges and concluded that he was allowed to get away with his unruly behavior when anxiety made him disruptive in public. At times, Ms. Thompson's marriage suffered, her own psychological health suffered, and she felt isolated as many caregivers do. Ms. Thompson experienced moments when it seemed impossible to carry on. But her message of empathy and hope lights the way through the pages of *The Silent Screaming*.

Through her own inner strength and the support of her husband, Ms. Thompson never lost focus on her mission as a mother: to make sure Joshua felt seen, heard, and loved. I highly recommend this book to all who are struggling to feel seen and heard themselves as the caregiver of a loved one with special needs.

Mary Alvarez, PhD, psychologist, Austin, Texas

HOW MANY TIMES?

How many times?

Asking myself this question was second nature, a reflex every time Joshua got in deep trouble. This time, I had rushed out of the airport terminal, having booked the first flight from New York City to Houston. Now I stood between two emotions—pure rage and fear. No parent or guardian expects to make an emergency trip to pick up an adult child in a jail cell lockdown. But there had been times I'd contemplated whether this day *would* finally come.

I have to get him out of jail was my one thought. Anger rushed in and along with it, the crawling, sticky nausea of fear.

I was afraid for Joshua's life (yes), and afraid for people around him (absolutely yes). But I couldn't just scream out the loudest fact I knew as his guardian: *Please listen. This young man has special needs. Stop what you're doing and listen.*

I thought, *he's going to be alone and isolated. He probably doesn't know why he's behind steel bars and surrounded by criminals. He can't explain his mental state.*

All these thoughts and more crossed my mind, because my twenty-year-old nephew, who had become my son, didn't have good judgment, or a clear sense of right or wrong.

Try explaining that to a stern-faced police officer. The expression "he doesn't know better" is lost on most defenders of the law. You can't explain in under a minute someone's moral compass, cognition, or their mental state. The police only knew part of the story when they answered the 911 call. Just hours before, Joshua had pulled a knife on my younger sister, Allison.

Whether that meant he simply held the blade or threatened to kill her (with Joshua not knowing the power of his words), I know it scared Allison. It cornered her into panic mode. It caused her to pick up the phone and dial.

More than a thousand miles away, sitting at a romantic dinner in New York City's Upper East Side, my husband and I were enjoying the kind of place where two adults can get lost in each other. Smiles over wine turned to deep sighs as my cell phone vibrated unanswered. Eric and I needed this time away. For our marriage and for each other, we needed to do some healing. The third time I heard that deep buzz in my purse, my stomach dropped.

Allison's voice sounded frayed and cracked.

"He was tased," she said. An electric pain shot through my chest, a cocktail mix of empathy and shock. The story unfolded and I held onto the edge of the dinner table. From the county jail to the smaller city jail, they had loaded Joshua up in the middle of the night, hauling him from one nightmare scene to the next. How horrible that must have felt, and how terrifying for them. I tried to see both sides of the coin. Anger brimmed at the surface. I knew Allison and Joshua, their dynamic. With their history of fighting almost like brother and sister, I didn't know how much was drama, histrionics, or the exact truth. One truth I did know for sure.

"You have to understand. Joshua *won't* hurt anyone," I cried at the front desk of the police station to the first person in sight who would listen.

Straight from a quiet dinner to a late-night flight toward Texas, I still wore the same clothes. I hadn't slept all night. I was sure my eyes were red from crying. I felt nearly stupefied from tension and lack of sleep.

One hand on the cold laminate police station counter and the other brushing back a flood of tears, I cast around for proof—some substantial evidence of Joshua's state. I dug through my purse for an old medicine bottle or a copy sheet of prescriptions, anything that would prove Joshua's condition as a special needs adult. I frantically called and recalled his therapist. I realized I was standing in the police station's lobby shouting, causing a public nuisance.

It would seem, then, *I* was the one needing help. Many families of special needs and the mentally ill know that feeling: emotions bleeding out, stress high, panic at code red. No one is listening, and *you* seem like the catalyst for trouble and chaos, *not* your loved one. I could only imagine what toll this had already taken on Joshua's mental state. He had been tased, tackled, handcuffed, shoved into a squad car, and locked in a damp, cold room. That picture is what drove me over the edge. We were both helpless in this moment.

What could I say? Joshua did not have just one set diagnosis for outsiders to recognize even vaguely—like autism, schizophrenia, or severe bipolar. I could not just say, "He's mentally ill and on medication." That ambiguity is lost on many people. I knew, inside that jail cell, my Joshua had a spectrum of mental illnesses, a whole history of *why*. These strangers could never know what a mother knows.

When a mother pleads for her child in a situation like this, she faces a wall of judgment. The person on the other side—in this case a blank-faced, stout male officer with his arms crossed in defense mode—has their own version of our story: "This man is twenty years old and a legal adult. He doesn't need you here." This creates the idea that I'm just another parent enabling their child's bad behavior, or that I'm trying to save his skin, or that I *want* to treat him like a child.

What they don't see is that the six-foot-three, two-hundred-pound young man—likely with his face buried in his hands—has the cognition and hastiness *of* a child. I knew this was a wake-up call for Joshua. Impulsively talking or lashing out comes with repercussions. Deep inside, he was just a little boy screaming, *Help me, please.* That became my final, whimpering cry at the police station. "Help us, please."

I felt silence close in. Not so much as a word back from the officer, and the other people in the station stared at me. Memories of Joshua, just a little boy standing and waving at me from the dirt road, flashed through my mind. I knew he didn't mean anyone harm. That knife in his hand, it was a real threat, sure, but one that he would never follow through. Reality began to take a new shift. *Will this be our life forever? How many times will I have to explain this, or be standing here in the future? How many times?*

❖❖❖

MY SISTER'S KEEPER

"Sometimes you will never know the value of a moment
until it becomes a memory. "

—*Dr. Seuss*

The year was 1973 on a gray, quiet afternoon in November when my baby sister came home. Thanksgiving dinner had just passed, and we had a new, sweet little family member to admire. I was four years of age. I looked at Tanya in her white wooden crib like any older sibling would—eyes wide with curiosity for this fresh, new, fragile life. She was another addition to our cramped blue and white trailer home with three other children and a single mother.

Our driveway ran between our trailer and my grandparents' house. Only now do I realize how important it was for us all to be close, huddled together on one plot of land in rural Pennsylvania. My mom needed the help. She had tragically lost my father one year prior and her inability to cope with that loss also led to her getting unexpectedly pregnant.

Nine months had passed in a blink. Mom brought Tanya home, such a tiny bundle, my baby sister. I touched her cheek and curled my finger under her wrinkly hand. Instinctively, I felt fiercely protective of her. *Who will take care of her? What is my job as a big sister now?* At such a tender age, these thoughts shuffled through me. I had no idea that one day I'd be the parent to her child, too.

I instinctively knew my role was nurturer and defender. *I am my sister's keeper.* It felt natural and wholesome to love her. If I had known then that I would one day be raising her son, my nephew Joshua, it would not have bothered me. Family was family to me, and the notion of acceptance ran deep. But not necessarily so with others around us. Even in these early, fledgling stages of my sister's life, I could feel a subtle air of rejection around her.

Half-sister. That word was so casually thrown about. It was always on the tip of people's tongues when they spoke about us as siblings. My older brother Robert, our younger sister Teresa, and I were one biological faction. Tanya was like the next generation, but a blood line over. Since we shared the same mother the term half-sister didn't mean much to me. We were still a family, and she was still my baby sister, little Tanya. Her birth father was shrouded in mystery. Unknown.

We had lost our father when Teresa was only a year old. He'd been killed in a car accident. Memories of the years that followed bleed together. Certain events stood out to me like faded snapshots. The summer that I was three, Teresa's first summer, I stepped through a glass window. A man I didn't know picked me up from a trail of blood and rushed me to the hospital. He may have been a neighbor. But young as I was, nothing was clear to me. Seasons and holidays passed. I remember my mother's belly became swollen with pregnancy. I was aware she was carrying another baby, but I had no idea how that could be.

Rumors began to buzz about my mother's instability. When I look back on it, I can imagine my mother's perspective: twenty-two years old with three children, and there's a knock on the door. The love of your life has been killed. How stable would you be? We all cope with grief and loss differently. For her, it might have been seeking comfort in the arms of another person, which resulted in a new life. I remember feeling very protective of my mom because everyone was talking about her and judging her. Interestingly, fifteen years later I would be judging her.

***

This did not lead to Tanya being given a good start. From the very beginning, her life seemed ill-fated. It started full of conflicting emotions:

a mingling of sadness, joy, and seething resentment. My paternal grandparents felt my mother had betrayed their son's memory, bringing a child into the world while everyone else sat in grief—even though he was not alive at the time she became pregnant. They attached this feeling of betrayal to Tanya.

People grieve along different spectrums—they might cry every day, mourn for months, or hold it in for years. My mother's measure of grief meant rolling with it and pushing on into the next big step. Little Tanya became a stereotype of the red-headed stepchild—unwanted and unruly—and that's exactly how she was treated. Differently, neglected, untouchable, untrustworthy, and less-than.

The confusion in her little face showed at times when those moments surfaced. Her eyes darted back and forth between all of us. Then she seemed to remember that she was the different one, the one with another father. Anxiety coiled inside me when I knew my paternal grandparents were coming for a visit, because Tanya would be singled out, shunned, and treated poorly. They would take us for ice cream and leave her behind. I hated that for her and for my mom. Tanya would make every effort to find her way into my grandmother's lap, only to be shooed away, told to move along, or go play. Her look of fear, rejection, and sad questioning haunted me for years.

How Tanya was viewed (half-sister, a scandal, a pariah) led to a real issue with her identity. So much hush-hush secrecy around her biological father complicated her self-worth. She wasn't allowed to know her past, but she could feel the unconscious shadows of it—almost like she was never supposed to be born in the first place. This proved to be a devastating way to start a life—not knowing who she was, who her father was, and everyone else watching her closely for any wrong move.

If Tanya's past or her father slipped into the conversation, the room suddenly dropped to a quiet standstill. It was the stuff of deep family secrets, and nobody wanted to talk about it. There was a sense of shame related to her even being in this world. Her sense of unworthiness became more and more evident in her teens and young adulthood. The way she presented and represented herself came out in her behavior first. It seemed to declare, "I don't care anymore."

Tanya didn't do well in school. She hung out with the wrong crowd. She tried to prove herself worthy of love, which led to her dressing provocatively: short skirts and low-cut shirts. Not that she got into a lot of trouble, but Tanya lived on the edge. Anything to gain that extra bit of attention she had lacked all her young life.

Tanya's life got to be rough. To speak truth, we all had a pretty rough childhood. Even before my father died, though he worked in a lumberyard, we lived on the edge of poverty. Survival was on a day-to-day basis. With our only main source of income now gone, we hauled our lives into an old metal trailer on my maternal grandparents' property. If it had not been for the two of them, we would not have survived. My mom was still so young with three kids and didn't stand a chance on her own.

When you live in a world of fear and scarcity, you don't necessarily realize it. Poverty carries a goldfish-in-a-bowl mentality. You have no idea anything better exists. So, we thought we had as normal a childhood as could be. Playing in dirt, making forts, and running freely in the yard, we did what all children of similar socioeconomic backgrounds of that time did.

We grew up in a very rural part of northwestern Pennsylvania. Our little town of Brockport had a population of only 1500. The next nearest town, Brockway, was approximately 3,000. Like many communities in sleepy, small-town America, there was one stoplight, one grocery store, and one post office. You could throw a rock and hit someone you knew. One elementary school, kindergarten to sixth grade, and one high school, seventh to twelfth grade, comprised the entire district. All of us were in one single pool of people we saw every day for years.

My exposure outside of that little world was limited. Our little rabbit-ear television had only three or four channels. Other than Saturday morning cartoons, we didn't have much screen time. Out of boredom, Tanya and I were often glued to each other as playmates and friends.

Psychologically and socially, we were made from different molds. I was the older, reliable sister, and she was the younger, insecure half-sister who didn't feel she had much ground to stand on. But she was never my shadow. She never followed in my footsteps. Her path was distinctly her own. One that caused people around town, in school, and at home to turn up their noses at the mere mention of her name.

I didn't understand the reasons why, but I knew. She knew. When the three of us older siblings traveled to New York on the invitation of our grandparents, Tanya was left behind. We typically traveled to New York for a few weeks during the summer. The reality was that my brother Robert was the favorite and the apple of my grandparents' eyes. He was their oldest son's son, and we girls were sometimes too much trouble—a wild pack of country girls! Nature and the outdoors were our playgrounds. We spent hours picking cherries and going for morning boat rides on the lake. My grandfather had a small fishing boat, and he would hesitantly allow Robert and me to go out with him and my uncle Joe in the clear, wide waters. It helped that I was a tomboy and wanted to be as close to my grandpa as possible. This made me feel closer to my dad, a sense of familiarity that Tanya had yet to experience. She had no idea what having a male authority figure felt like since she lived under the wing of protective women.

On the other hand, my maternal grandmother made the best effort she could. Tanya was "one of the kids" back in Pennsylvania. Looking back, I could see how differently my little sister had been treated, and I harbored some guilt. The image of her sitting at home while the rest of us spent time on the lake, running through the cherry orchard and the vineyard, or traipsing through the countryside, still sits on me like a bad dream. Those will never be memories she shares with us as siblings. I thought of her sitting on the porch, chin in her hands, waiting for someone to come home and explain the fun we'd had. I could imagine her asking, "Where did you go? What did you get to see? When do I get to come?"

When any of us asked why, our questions were met with nervous gestures and coughs. *Why*, I still asked inside. The playful little girl I knew darting across the yard would one day become my Joshua's mother. She would become a source of pain, anger, annoyance, frustration, and resentment. But in the end, she was still a worthy human being, and she was still my sister. I would keep her close, try to see her when no one else would, and listen to her voice screaming from inside.

❖❖❖

TWO

A FAMILY DIVIDED

"All happy families are alike,
but every unhappy family is unhappy in its own way."

—*Leo Tolstoy*

Days in the Pennsylvania countryside are green, breezy, and lazy, but full of adventures.

It was 1975-1976 when my mother remarried a man named Pete—a retired, strict, stern Marine. After living on the marine base in Virginia for a short time, we moved into a doublewide trailer on the other side of Brockway, next to a farm.

One Sunday afternoon Pete took us to the local cattle auction and purchased us a pony. I don't remember who came up with the name, but we named the pony Sugar Babe. The family next door owned a long, wide pasture and a handful of livestock. We had a handshake deal with them that we were allowed to use their barn for our new, sweet horse. But my memories surrounding Sugar Babe turned to loss, confusion, heartache, and a new family divide.

Our lives changed forever on a thick summer day in the pasture. The neighbors, an older couple, had a young man living with them to help take care of the farm. He was an uneducated, somewhat unkempt southern man named Tim. He'd look at all of us blankly—but at my married mother of four with a special kind of glimmer. The kind of a look children notice but don't quite understand. One bright afternoon, the four of us kids huddled around and saddled up Sugar Babe. Tanya squirmed as she waited for her turn, her first ride. The day she first sat on a horse was the day our mother decided to walk out.

There's no way to describe the memory of a parent leaving—unreal, frozen, forever spread across time in slow motion. If this event happens at an age of awareness—for me, at six years of age—you don't forget it. Dressed (unusual in itself) and with a bounce in her step, my mom sashayed out onto the front porch and set down a vinyl suitcase. Without a goodbye, she looked over almost as if to study each one of us in the moment, picked up the luggage again, and walked off alongside Tim, the neighbors' help, who also clutched a suitcase.

"Their mother ran away with the neighbor," was one small-town sentence in the rumor mill that was entirely the truth. The actuality of those words didn't hit me right away. As we watched our mother walk away with a new man, my thoughts didn't register any kind of scandal or love affair between these two. Sure, there'd been a spark, but we didn't know how hot. The first words that rushed through my head haunted me for years. *What is going to happen to us? What is going to happen to Tanya?*

How could this kind of abandonment happen? I believe it goes back to where we lived. In our small town, the life paths were narrow. Grow up, find a mate, get married, and have children—unless the plans are to be a teacher. None of us could imagine attending college, let alone someone paying for it. Sometimes "marry, make babies, stay" was said aloud. Other times it was simply a known rule, deeply embedded in the community.

Already a mother as a teen, Mom had worked odd jobs as a waitress, a caregiver for an elderly person, anything she could find. Each of us began to feel the effects of being the poor kids—the ones who couldn't afford dance lessons, or nice school clothes, or satchels. This was no secret to others. We didn't even own a car. Our dreams, goals, or fantasies of a richer life were stifled under the weight of surviving each day. Having a roof over our heads, each our portion for dinner—that was more important than acquiring the "next best thing" any other kid in class wanted. My mother bringing in any kind of paycheck was crucial in our income bracket, and finding a partner (and hence, a double income) always seemed like the better bet.

My grandmother, who worked in a factory, would nudge me and say, "Rhonda, you don't have to be this just because everyone else is." I had no idea the impact and influence that one remark would have on the rest of my life.

Deep down, I wanted to believe I had the power to break that chain. As a straight-A student—one who didn't have a single red mark or problem in school—I naturally loved to learn. My other siblings seemed to fall into another category. But in certain ways, I did take the traditional path. Getting my high school diploma and an engagement ring on the same day, it seemed I was set up to stay in this one-way street of a town forever.

Before that, going back to me as a six-year-old girl, I got mixed signals of how a woman should act. A lot of this influence came from my mother—who ping-ponged between child-rearing and going missing. This made me a nurturer archetype from an early age. If my own mother could not be there to save us, then who? Me? That day at the pasture, I looked at my three-year-old sister Tanya, blissfully unaware, sitting atop the horse. This memory would trigger quite an emotional ride.

Throughout Tanya's first three years, I tried to give her a voice and circumvent her being treated differently. For a short while, we had a little more stability and a roof over our heads when my mother partnered with Pete, our ex-Marine stepfather. We came to realize she did this for convenience, a little cash in the bucket. Now, two years into the marriage, this is where all of us stood: watching our mother walk out the door with the next-door neighbor.

No one expected it would be with Tim. He was originally from Tennessee, so he had a southern accent, long, disheveled hair, and often wore a dirty, tattered bandana. He was the opposite of clean-cut Pete, who (as you might imagine) was very structured, coming from the Marines. I think my mom rebelled against so much rigidity, and it attracted her to Tim's lax nature. I think she wanted to escape her reality of routine, and Tim could help her do that with the snap of a finger, as he was a transient kind of fellow. He was the type to hitchhike, to move along, and mosey through life.

What's going to happen to us? What's going to happen to Tanya? It was my first thought, watching our mother's ghostly figure get smaller and smaller down the road. Looking back, I think, *Why was I so concerned about Tanya, and not everyone else?* My little sister's welfare—not my own survival—thrust itself to the front of my mind. As we silently put Sugar Babe away in the barn, we paced back and forth over the yard. The sun sank, the day inched by into darkness. I am not sure how, but I found the phone number of the glass plant where my grandmother worked and told her we were alone and what had happened. She told me to lock the door and she would get there as soon as she could explain to her boss and drive to where we were.

I called a neighbor as soon as I hung up the phone with Grandma. "We're alone. Can you watch us?" The neighbor came immediately and stayed with us until our grandmother arrived thirty minutes later. She had us pack a change of clothes. We piled into her car and holed up in her house like it was the Apocalypse—fearful, on edge, not knowing the next move.

Some children might be okay with this sudden "permission" to run wild. They might see it as freedom. But instinctively we knew it was not. Nothing about true abandonment feels like freedom. It feels like panic, disorder, and a sudden loss of structure.

The next day my grandmother began calling family members to determine who could help and where each of us would be staying. My paternal grandfather in New York immediately said he would take Robert. One of my aunts said she would take Teresa, and I would stay with Grandma. She spent hours on the phone trying to figure out who could take three-year-old Tanya.

We need to make sure Tanya has a house, my thoughts repeated in a loop, and finally got spoken out loud: "We need to make sure Tanya has a house." This was my first real memory of thinking I had to be her voice because she didn't have one. The abandonment, rehousing, and that swift call-to-action inside my mind created a piercingly emotional time for me.

When people ask me about leadership and servanthood mentality,

I think that was the first time I experienced it. It was natural, ingrained in my thought process, like an instinct. Only six years old, and my mind took control of the situation. But my grandmother took over the logistics of "who goes where" and how each of us would survive this.

For decades, I harbored anger for my mother. Nothing could make me understand why she would leave with all of us standing and watching. Through therapy, I was finally able to stand in her shoes. To say that our stepfather Pete was an incredibly controlling husband was an understatement. He was the stereotype of a hardcore Marine. Tall, sturdy, reddish-blonde hair cut short, you'd never catch him with a hair out of place, let alone a beard. His hardworking nature made for stability, but he was cold, unforgiving, and harsh on my mother. I learned to let empathy seep in. She had walked through fire and continually burned herself through partnerships—trying to cope.

I remembered that day in the pasture as if it were a scene from a *Lifetime Movie Network* film. Standing in the grass, my legs shook. I couldn't believe what I saw. Without a wave, a smile, or anything, Mom glanced back at us from a distance.

Even though we had temporary housing with my grandmother, none of us knew what the next few weeks and months would look like. It was "the great divide"—when siblings are forced to split up.

Teresa, a short little tomboy of a girl, ended up with Dorothy, my mother's sister. Robert went far away to my paternal grandparents in New York. I stayed with my maternal grandparents, and Tanya ended up with my grandma's sister Harriet, who no one either liked or hated. We just didn't want to be around her. And Tanya got the bottom of the barrel.

Aunt Harriet and Uncle Fred were strict and not a traditional loving and warm couple. Showing very little emotion and empathy, they were a stern and hard-to-love pair, but Tanya needed the structure—and more importantly, a home.

The environment was critical and harsh, and Tanya already the "untouchable" or "pariah" of the family. It didn't make her life any easier. Although Robert lived in another state, Teresa and I were somewhat side-by-side in our little town. Tanya lived fifteen minutes away, but to her three-year-old mind, this must have registered thousands of miles. She must have felt she was being punished, isolated, or given up. Truth be told, she just didn't know the reasons why. No toddler would. I can't psychoanalyze her, but undoubtedly this was a traumatizing event causing her to feel unwanted, unseen, and unheard once more. She must have thought, *Where is my mother? She doesn't say goodnight anymore. Am I being punished, and that's why she's gone?*

When siblings are split apart, it's a soul-breaking experience. Insecurity rises emotionally, physically, and financially. The pillars of everyday life shift. Children must recreate their idea of family and connection.

Even though we lived at the poverty level, the four of us still had had a life together, and we'd done sibling things all the time. Suddenly, that simple countryside life together was gone. The old metal swing set that our grandparents bought us sat empty. I kept going back to images of us roughhousing in the dirt, making mud pies, and being creative because we didn't own bikes or skates to allow us to roam. We did typical fun and even naughty things together before the divide. Even in a time-out, all four of us had to stay put—together—in separate corners. Old memories suddenly felt dearer, more a part of me than ever.

Once, we'd decided to pour several boxes of cornflakes on the kitchen floor, only to run and jump into them as if there were autumn leaves! Another time, we took that up a notch, poured a bag of flour down the hallways, and ran, slid, and tumbled through it as if it were a patch of snow. Laughs and giggles echoed through the house. Our mother looked at us with an evil eye. Typical childhoods are full of bad and good times, and one day, you grow up. In our case, it happened faster.

Now that we lived in four separate corners, heaviness began to weigh us down. Each of us dealt with being alone and isolated, feeling like an only child. I wandered through the silence of my grandparents' house, running my hands up the walls in boredom. My eye caught the bathroom mirror, and the memory burned permanently into my mind. I saw a little girl a head taller than others my age, with wispy, short dark hair, and big, icy blue eyes.

What I saw should have been the face of an innocent child. In the sound of the water whistling down the faucet, and in the dry mildewy air, I felt the rotten, uncomfortable nature of this bathroom for more than one reason. I avoided this room like a sickness. I ignored the memories it kept and continued trying to believe this was as normal, stable, and happy as my life could be.

The idea of "disparity" and truly being different from other families financially, socially, and emotionally didn't happen until much later as I grew into my preteen years. At school, I noticed my classmates come in with new book bags or pencil holders while mine stayed the same. I also distinctly remember realizing this difference one day when my grandmother and I surfed through the clothing racks at Goodwill. It was definitely not where other kids bought their starchy, clean jeans, new sneakers, and backpacks. The concept of money and lack thereof started to register then at age nine or ten: *Gosh, we really are different.*

The fact we didn't have a car told the truth. Grandma drove us everywhere. Mom and Tim came back after about nine months, and we kids moved back in with them. But even then, Grandma took us wherever we needed to go.

We did not have neighbor kids and friends and could not leave the country, so to speak. I didn't have best friends to walk over and see because it was the sticks, the middle of nowhere. Kids I went to school with either lived in town, or they too lived in the outskirts of their own worlds. Isolation was a part of life, and even more so when I ambled through my grandmother's house, for the most part, alone.

Food is always another sign of one's level of poverty. I suddenly realized we drank boxed milk, and that we didn't buy potatoes and peel them. Mashed potatoes came from cardboard boxes, and our fridge had a big, gooey block of cheddar cheese. None of those things registered until I realized how other kids ate and compared it with how we did.

Any additional money given to us, my grandmother spent on the basics. She used that money for the trailer payment, the electric bill, and everything down to the penny. Sometimes, my mind ran through a scenario where we might have been living in a house with no electricity or running water—like squatters or homeless people.

Mom walking away from our lives had created a positive: a seed of independence and survival in me—a spirit that wanted to take care of everybody, even though my brother Robert was older than me and in second grade in New York. That's not to say I was more mature at six or seven years old, but my sense of being grounded came earlier. This was the foundation of who I would be as an adult—through those early years as a bright child in honors classes who didn't have trouble at school. Doing my homework kept my mind off my home life. It was one thing I could control.

All my siblings struggled with grades and fell into their own story-lines of grief, abandonment, and trying to cope. Each of us remembers that day in the pasture with a different narrative—shocked, afraid, or in a hazy state of doubt. That's the angle of split siblings and a broken family system. Each person has their trauma, one piece of the shattered glass, and it never quite fits together again no matter how you rehash the story. Tanya only knew she was already a wild card and never fit in anyway. When I think back on us siblings getting split apart, my little sister already had the mentality that she was on the outskirts of her family, always pushed halfway out the door, already out in left field. It was as if she said, "Don't you all see me? Don't you hear me? No. I didn't think so."

❖❖❖

THREE

WALKING OUT

"Yesterday I was clever, so I wanted to change the world.
Today I am wise, so I am changing myself."

—*Rumi*

Walking across the graduation stage felt like a big, deep exhale. *Finally, this part is over.* Our group of roughly eighty students and their parents and relatives filled the room with a roar of applause. I graduated with honors and my grandparents, sitting in the fold-up chairs, glowed with pride. Grandma always said this would be my destiny.

"Study hard, Rhonda. You're bigger than this town." In a small town, celebrations can feel big. To me, this really did feel like the beginning.

A few friends and I decided to have a last-minute graduation party at my house. Because we lived in the middle of nowhere, we thought we could get away with just about anything, even a little rowdy fun and a few drinks.

Right before the small get-together, though, my boyfriend Ryan showed up with a big question: "Will you marry me, Rhonda?"

Although my teenage self believed I loved him, I didn't really say yes. I actually put the ring, still in its box, on top of the refrigerator. Growing up in that area, I knew marriage was the next step, what seemed destined for me. But something didn't feel right. My grandmother's influential words echoed in my mind.

Throughout my high school years, I lived as an outsider, or maybe I just wanted to *be* on the outside. I wasn't a rebel like Tanya, nor was I a person with a steady, set path. Marrying at eighteen, getting pregnant a few months later, and staying in our slow town watching the paint dry and life go by were things other girls did. I was more interested in getting good grades than in being part of the popular group. But I had no idea what life beyond the school bell looked like.

Much of my genetic imprint and environmental influences centered around marriage and babies, so I fell into our town's cliché lifestyle quickly. Two years after graduation and an up and down relationship with Ryan, I succumbed to going out on a date with my neighbor, Richard. He had been "in love" with me for years and something about it seemed safe. It didn't take long until I married him, the boy next door. It hit me: *Just like Mom married our neighbor, Tim.*

Finding a partner in the boy next door was not an uncommon theme in our small town. Richard was a few years older than I, a small-town woodsman who loved to hunt and trap. He wasn't what I pictured as an "until death do us part" husband, but it was the trajectory a girl in my shoes took, despite my ambitions to leave. Richard had been giving me bedroom eyes since I was an early teen. Once, he'd slipped me an eight-or-nine-page love letter on notebook paper, scrawled with promises and sweet nothings.

On reflection, this relationship drew me in because it represented security, normalcy, and familiarity. *This guy really loves me,* I thought. *It's been years, so it must be real.*

Dating felt natural, mainly because I already knew him so well. My whole family knew him, and oddly, he became a regular at our kitchen table—for dinner, sometimes breakfast or coffee. He had spent a great deal of time at our house even when I was only a child, but I never connected any kind of attention then to marriage.

In 1989, when I was two years out of school, Richard and I married in a small ceremony after a six-month engagement. The wedding was held at the small local Methodist church with immediate family and the reception at the local town hall.

Our honeymoon phase didn't last long. Still trying to figure out my next move career-wise, I worked two jobs: one as a waitress and the other selling used cars. The second was an odd job for a woman at that time, but getting commissions and putting away money became the best springboard *out*. Deep in my heart, I knew this marriage had an expiration date. I just didn't know when to leave or what to do.

By this time in 1991, my sister Tanya had birthed a son, my nephew Joshua. My nurturing for her naturally transferred to her son, and he was already partially in my care.

One afternoon as Joshua slept in his car seat in the dealership's office, my high school best friend Michelle poked her head into my office. Over a pot of old coffee, we talked about each other's futures.

"You care for people all the time, Rhonda," She chimed in. It was a lightning bolt moment. "You really should think about going into nursing."

Since I was so desperate to point an arrow on the path—to have some direction, to leave, to get out, anything—I thought more deeply about it. Soon after, I turned in my application to nursing school. It wasn't long before an acceptance letter landed in my hand. This was my ticket out!

At the same time, the marriage posed another kind of mental and emotional struggle—I had two-step children with Richard, both of which I had adopted. Yes, it was a legal adoption. They were quite young when this happened. Leaving them gave me a huge sense of guilt, and I didn't want to endanger their security, either. I wondered if this was how my mother felt so many years ago.

In the midst of this dilemma—stay or leave—Tanya gave birth to Joshua. Born on the edge of my marriage and into an uncertain future, he came screaming into the world. His name was Joshua Lloyd after our maternal grandfather, and I loved him from the second I held him. Wrapping him tighter in his swaddle after his birth, I handed him back to Tanya. Something about that made me shudder, the way she reluctantly, hesitantly received him. I knew she, too, felt unsure about being a mother.

For the first few years of his life, Joshua was mostly in my care. Looking back, I figure that it probably wasn't good for an infant to be around so much marital strife. Though we didn't fight, Richard became controlling and obsessed with constantly needing to know my whereabouts. Knowing I wanted to leave made him especially clingy and irritable. The stress of being continually hounded by him piled up on me, and even at such a tender age, Joshua must have felt the tense atmosphere. The marriage finally dissolved.

A therapist helped me work through my feelings of fear about the world out there—what it looked like outside of marriage, and how subconsciously scared I had become of displeasing Richard. *How do I get out of this? How do I survive it?* I needed to know. Expressing my emotions always seemed to make him fly off the handle, and I knew a decision like this would leave him livid. Richard was a hunter, trapper, and taxidermist. He wasn't timid when it came to being forceful.

I tried to push aside the fears, and the stars began to align. The day my marriage effectively ended was the day I got my acceptance letter to nursing school. I went to Richard to share the good news and he snapped back, "Listen Rhonda, you cannot be a student, a wife, and a mother, so you have to make your choice."

Knowing that he had already established my roles for me really snapped the cord. I walked out the door and into fresh judgment from the community around me. They felt I had abandoned my two stepchildren, though I didn't see it that way. I loved these kids and took care of them, but ultimately this was *his* life. I realized he didn't care too much for mine.

Just like so many times I remembered throughout childhood and teens, I packed my bags once again. Clothes, shoes, any of the bare necessities. I squeezed my life into a duffle bag. The old memories were left behind, and it was time to make new ones. Life, in under a day, changed, though I knew some things would stay the same. Little Joshua and I had each other. I held him closer, dearer, and looked forward to what would happen next. Our lives entwined. But each of us would have our own story in time.

❖❖❖

MOVING ON

"You don't have to see the whole staircase,
just take the first step."

—*Martin Luther King Jr.*

M y new apartment began to feel like home. It took a little bit of creativity: some thrift store furniture, odds and ends of décor, and anything cobbled together to start my life as a single woman *and* nursing student. I lived with Michelle in the upstairs of a small house a mile from the college. She was in her second year of nursing school, and it created some security for me to live with someone I knew. The A&P textbooks and half-empty coffee mugs definitely said this place was lived in around the clock by students.

It felt even more hectic when I had a toddler running in circles on the carpet. Joshua came to visit me often during my college days. Those days were bright, happy, full of first giggles and facial expressions from him. We made memories together. Some days, we fed ducks at the pond and had carefree, fun days away from my bustling academic life.

The University of Pittsburgh at Bradford, sitting in lush woods in the far northwest part of the state, was just over an hour from where I grew up. Back home, my grandmother had started taking care of Joshua one day a week. Then it became two days, three, four, and pretty much a full-time job. Tanya grew more and more elusive. Her whereabouts, job prospects, and plans for the future were mostly kept secret from the rest of us. Our grandmother passively accepted this. So did I. For a time, Tanya lived in Lockhaven with Joshua's dad—Josh's—family, and I would drive three hours to see Joshua.

Visiting Joshua or having him over to my place became routine. I squeezed these visits into my schedule between classes and work. I often felt like a single parent! Something about Joshua's biological father, Josh, never had sat right with me. He looked right through Joshua almost like he was invisible and not a flesh-and-blood child with needs. It didn't seem to me that Josh really wanted to be with Tanya, either, or she with him. When I saw them together, he appeared disengaged, his attention on anything else. That was one thing he and Tanya started to have in common—increasing absence both physically and emotionally. Little scenarios began to play in my head about Joshua in danger—falling down the stairs, or turning on the stove, or any number of hazards toddlers run into.

Who would be there for him? I started to stress about Joshua the same as I had about Tanya as a baby. The parallel was uncanny. *Who is going to be there?*

Until that point, Joshua had met all his pediatric milestones—walking, running, picking up small objects, and saying lots of basic words. He had a normal build for his age. He had blondish-brown hair, round cheeks, and explosive energy. Early on, he also had a passion and empathy for animals. Horses. They were his obsession! One day while visiting, I plopped him on a horse, Misty, just as I had done with Tanya on Sugar Babe so long ago in the pasture. We captured the moment in a photo. It was a sweet memory, and he still talks about it today.

Watching the light in his eyes gave me hope this kid would have a lot of joy to look forward to. But then during late 1993 and early 1994, my grandmother's phone calls to me began to cause a twinge of worry. The sound of her voice was unsure, quiet, and she would clear her throat as if uncomfortable with what she'd be saying about him. Joshua's behavior had deteriorated more than what seemed normal for an unruly toddler being bounced around between my grandparents and Tanya.

One day Grandma called me and struggled to get out the words.

"Rhonda, I think we have a problem with him."

Although he'd already been potty trained, Joshua started to lose control of his bowels. Accidents became regular events. No matter how many times my grandmother urged him to try, re-training became a lost cause. *Well, that just doesn't seem normal. Something isn't right.* As a nursing student, I didn't need to be told twice to take him to a doctor.

I rang Tanya from home that weekend to set up a doctor's appointment for Joshua. On the third unanswered call, I gave up. I had no way of finding my sister. I drove up to her shabby white rental house and knocked on the door. Over the years, Tanya had been hard to tie down. She moved every few months, and I had no clue if I was at her door or a stranger's.

Thankfully, Joshua was with my grandmother, and we took the initiative to take him for a check-up. The three of us waited patiently for his exam to end. After a lot of prodding, probing, and sighs, the doctor told us what he'd found. Nothing could have prepared us for those words.

"It looks like Joshua has lost much of the muscle tenacity in his rectum." The doctor broke off, knowing the next part would hurt us. "Although it's not for certain, it appears this was by force, through abuse of some kind. Abuse that's likely been recurring and violent."

Trying to process these words, my first emotion came up—rage. Blind, white-hot rage. Out of all the scenarios I had worried about with Joshua as a toddler, the idea that someone would molest him had never run through my mind. *Who? Who was it?* I wanted to know, but at the same time, I understood Tanya would never talk. I had no way to know who had been around him, where Tanya might have taken him, or what strangers had been introduced into their house. I was distraught, as was my grandmother. When I did finally tell Tanya the diagnosis, she shut the conversation down as quickly as it came.

"Nothing. Nothing happened!"

Tanya couldn't come up with any other reasonable explanation why her three-year-old child had suddenly lost his muscle control, either. Her excuses came with shrugs and dry denials of any knowledge.

By this time Tanya had another child, Anna, and neither my grandmother nor I wanted to be the ones to tear apart her family. More than a year passed before my grandmother learned from one of her glass plant colleagues that she had seen Joshua on multiple occasions at a different house in Brockway. It didn't take us long to figure out who it was. It's a person I can't reveal now. When we confronted Tanya, she continued to deny anything had happened. Calling Child Protective Services was at that time something of a taboo, and my grandparents were not about to call attention to the family in that negative way. How anyone could allow this to happen to a three-year-old was beyond us.

Many years later, when Joshua was deep into psychotherapy, the therapist would explain that this was the epicenter of Joshua's psychiatric disorders. Physically, he had been damaged down there. Psychologically, he was trying to separate his body from what had happened. When a child goes through sexual trauma, bowel movements become a means to escape the pain, the inherent feeling of that action being entirely "wrong," and the body disassociates. With the real truth out there on "how and why," we only knew it was best just to keep Joshua regular— with potty training, a schedule, and going to school.

Once, I remember him sitting on the red plastic potty I kept at my college apartment for the weekends he came, and Joshua paused to say, "I'm doing my exercises."

I knew that "exercises" meant what the doctor suggested: Kegels, to gain back his muscle tenacity. Squeezing and letting go, he listened to instructions carefully. It was almost like he knew how important it was to reverse this, and to go back to a normal feeling down there. The temptation to just ask, probe who, what, and when always rose up, but the psychiatrist told us, "Don't pressure him. It could make it worse."

Final exams crept up on me that spring in 1994. The desire to graduate, get out, and move up in the world came full blossom. Along with that, I rekindled a connection with a guy I'd met while waitressing in 1991. A sweet, stable man named Eric who, on occasion, had also worked at the restaurant. We'd developed a friendship, and he always listened to the hard, confusing times at home while I was still married to Richard. During those days of working together with him, while also getting the therapy I needed to finally leave my controlling husband, I knew intuitively I would spend the rest of my life with Eric. We started dating the summer of 1992, before school. Seven or eight months into the relationship, we knew this would become a serious union.

"After you graduate, do you want to move to Seattle with me?" Eric asked, waiting for my answer on the telephone. I curled my finger over the cord.

I wanted to scream *yes!* Seattle, Washington—a flourishing, hip city with plenty of young professionals, job opportunities, a chance to really *live* out there, and do it with someone I love—it was a dream. Though moving up in the world came with guilty thoughts of leaving my heart behind. With Joshua still in my grandmother's house ninety percent of the time, we still had our little weekends together.

In my college apartment, I heard my nephew laugh and watched him scuttle across the carpet with his toy cars. Every single second that I had to pay attention to him, to watch him, was crucial to me. *Who else will do this when I'm gone?* I thought, as Joshua babbled a few new words. *Who will watch him grow?* Joshua laid his head across my lap. *Who will listen to him talk, laugh, scream?* Someone had to.

❊❊❊

FIVE

STARTING A FAMILY

"The family you come from is important,
but the family you create is your number one priority."
—*Anonymous*

Thinking about the day I left comes easy. It's an image burned into memory—one I've seen every day for almost thirty years. Driving slowly on the dirt driveway by my grandma's trailer, I glance behind my shoulder. In a red and blue Superman t-shirt and the underpants which we worked so hard to get him to use again—Joshua holds up a hand. He's still waving even though I know he can't see me in the car. I'm leaving, and he's holding on.

On the lawn, I see his little bare feet. No father to stand by him with a reassuring hand. Josh, his biological father—God knew where he had gone. During those months, I never trusted Josh or Tanya. And after leaving for Seattle, it would be even harder to. The grief of separation, severe anxiety, guilt—all these emotions flooded in. *What if I should stay?* Even at the eleventh hour, with my apartment all packed up and some of my boxes already shipped, I broke down several times with second thoughts. *What if he thinks I left him for good?* I sat in the airport, my little dog in my lap for comfort, still second-guessing myself. My friend's words echoed in my mind, "You have to go, Eric is waiting for you."

I knew that at three years old, Joshua didn't have awareness of time or distance. Saying I would be back *some* and not *every* weekend was lost on him. For all he knew, moving to Washington state might have meant moving just a town over, not more than two-thousand miles away. Once in Seattle, I got word Joshua was with my grandparents as often as before. That made me sigh in relief. I kept my promise to come back some weekends. Every four months or so, I flew back and spent every waking second with Joshua. Each time, he looked bigger, taller, and more stretched out. He had less "baby fat" than the toddler I knew.

Rarely did I ever see Tanya or Josh when I visited. They were more and more out of the picture. Each time I came back, I was disturbed to notice a new Joshua emerge through his personality and face—a distance in his eyes, like a little lost boy. It frightened me to think what he thought of or remembered but couldn't say. From those days on, it haunted me, and I wondered what haunted him.

Eric and I settled into newlywed life. We married a year after I moved to Seattle, on October 4th, 1995, in a private ceremony on the island of St. Croix. Although we invited all our families, no one attended. But that was fine by us. It rained all day on the island, so we had to make some modifications and in lieu of a beach wedding, we got married in an old sugar mill. We spent the next couple of days on the cruise ship heading back to Miami. It is interesting how Eric and I taking our vows alone and isolated would resemble much of our lives to come—absolutely on our own.

There were few or no nursing jobs at this time in the early '90's so I started my career working in a nursing home. I could never have imagined how much I would love nursing. In my first experience of caring for those who resembled my beloved grandmother, I knew I was meant to be a nurse. I was meant to take care of others.

Nearly two years went by, and Houston, Texas called our name to be our next new home. Along with a big move, two new jobs, and finding good housing, Eric and I were also ready to level up our marriage through the next step in the American Dream—starting a family. Before our courtship, we both knew we wanted children, at least one or two. Back then we hadn't been ready to make that commitment. But after trying for a few months, that big, happy family fantasy began to feel like a nightmare.

Each month there came another hard "no" on a pregnancy test. Like any woman, I questioned what was wrong with me. I had done everything "right" before making this decision—having a steady foundation, both of us with excellent professional lives, a strong marriage, a home—but my body felt like a living embodiment of all that was "wrong." Soon enough, I began to look back on that image of little Joshua in the road—waving, growing distant, and disappearing. How could both of my sisters—who each had three children—have no problem bearing babies they didn't have the means to support? I had the means but couldn't get pregnant!

After a year trying the old-fashioned way, each month a "no" with all the emotion to accompany it, both Eric and I went through infertility testing. Not only did I have issues with an abnormal cycle and spotty ovulation, but Eric had a low sperm count. We did three artificial inseminations without success and moved on to the next option. A specialist suggested Eric see a urologist who could perform a minor procedure that would increase his sperm count and motility. The procedure was called a varicocelectomy, and Eric had mixed feelings about it. But he wanted to do whatever he needed to for us to have a baby. We also felt some guilt about a pregnancy we lost right after I moved to Seattle and were determined to have a second chance.

After that option failed, we did one more artificial insemination before the breaking point. Many couples struggling with infertility reach the plateau where they've exhausted all resources trying to move up before they move on. The pressure of having a child began to feel so overwhelming it took over our entire relationship. I was the one obsessively thinking about it, though, more so than Eric.

My thoughts began to echo daily, *I need to have a baby, I need to have a baby,"* almost like it was another achievable goal such as graduating or getting a job. Something I could do if I worked hard enough. This time, I couldn't put my work ethic or heart into this. It was black and white. Pregnant or not. Again, those thoughts of comparison came up. I had two younger sisters, neither of them married or with steady jobs, who seemed to get pregnant by mere touch!

Punishment—that's what I decided was the culprit beyond my fertility issues—*what am I being punished for and why?* I had guilt for leaving Joshua, and I shuffled through "what-ifs" and "Maybe if we had tried earlier in the marriage." All these scenarios and doubts came up. That's the point where most couples need to hear the final truth.

Sitting in the physician's office, I glanced over at Eric. He looked placid, almost peaceful, slowly nodding along to the doctor's words. I knew my husband wasn't necessarily an introvert. Like many men, he's not eager to go through rigorous testing or raise his hand to talk during a therapy appointment. His feelings, though there, felt locked away from me. The doctor talked on with a tone of condolence,

"I'm sorry. We could try (this) or (that) again, but it's unlikely to work."

Emotion in the room thickened, and tears welled up in my eyes. Next to me, Eric sat blank-faced. This created in me a storm of resentment, and I wanted to scream. *You should be crying too! Why aren't you crying? We can't have a baby! Do you hear what they're telling us right now?*

This journey was not entirely hopeless, however, and we did finally see an in vitro fertilization specialist, but God knows those treatments aren't exactly cheap. Although established in our careers, Eric and I were not in a financial or an emotional position to place $12,000 on a procedure that would likely fail. Finally, we said to each other, "We have to stop. We can try again later, but right now we have to stop."

That voice inside to "try again, fail, try again" began to slowly subside, but it never fully disappeared. To my mind, being a mother at some point and living in a small town was just something expected of a woman. I had no idea it would be a focal point of even more expectation, especially when I desired to be a mother. Over the next few months, that image of three-year-old Joshua on the road, waving 'bye, started to come up in my dreams more and more. In a way, I felt like his presence was calling me. Both he and I wanted the same things deep down inside, a family, a sense of belonging, and for our voice to be heard.

✣✣✣

A FEW DAYS OR FOREVER

"When life changes to be harder,
change yourself to be stronger."

—*Anonymous*

One of my last images of my grandfather is of an old man, face wrinkled with so many memories, seated at the kitchen table in his trailer. Old, thick road maps were spread across the wood, and his fingers—ragged, tan, boney—tracked the miles from Brockport to Seattle, and Brockport to Houston. Back in the '90s, in the days before GPS or Google, owning a big, heavy map was a necessity for some, and almost a pastime for others like my retired grandfather. He was so excited to show me how many fewer miles I would be away from home.

Although a lot of memories of him are spoiled, deeply ingrained in my subconscious, I cherished those moments when my grandpa showed emotions. His Depression-era generation did not do that often, and it was interesting to see his face brighten at such a simple thought. A year and a half after we moved to Houston, he had a heart attack and got rushed to the Pittsburgh hospital for a quadruple bypass.

I got the call at work and booked a flight an hour later. It was a surprise to my grandfather when I ran into the ICU at Shadyside Hospital in Pittsburgh. He spoke his last words that day: "You little devil." Not long after that, my grandmother and I made the difficult decision to turn off his ventilator.

The next few days would be full of funeral plans, flowers from friends and family, and the entire swamp of planning that no one expects to do while in grief. My grandmother, of course, was more upset than I.

Watching Tanya walk into the funeral home with Joshua in tow created mixed emotions for me, even more than what I was already feeling. Joshua immediately ran into my arms, and I remember the smell of little boy sweat, a child who had worked up so much happy energy it seeped from his very pores. His attitude was pure sunshine, but the world around him looked grim. Tanya and Josh had moved back to Brockway and by this time their relationship was even rockier.

I knew my grandmother needed and wanted to take care of Joshua more than ever now. I didn't want her to be alone. After the funeral ceremony, I stood alone staring down into the casket, touching his cold, lifeless hand and telling him I loved him. "I forgive you," the words welled up like tears, and they were memories of my childhood swallowed down, pushed aside, but secrets only he and I knew. Those would be words shared just between the two of us.

Now spending most of her days alone with Joshua, although still taking him back and forth to Tanya, my grandmother started to reassess her situation. *How can I do this with a small child?* Since she had never traveled or set foot on a plane, we agreed she should come to Houston for a visit. The kicker was doing that with a nearly six-year-old boy who was rambunctious and eager to travel, too!

Grandma took that scenario in stride. "Why not? Let's do it!" Joshua, by this time, had been in several different schools and placed on Ritalin. He was inquisitive and energetic but was lacking some educational fundamentals.

My grandmother accepted he was struggling. But she didn't want to admit that what he'd experienced at age three would have permanent implications for his life. I still imagined the sweet little boy who I kissed and hugged goodbye three years earlier. I wanted, as much as my grandmother, for him still to be an innocent little boy.

After eying him awhile in the kitchen, I noticed some peculiar behavior, particularly around food. He'd constantly sneak into the pantry or refrigerator. Eating was almost an obsession, a psychological urge to binge, to eat as much as he could in one sitting. "Slow down" and "You'll spoil your dinner" became my regular phrases. What it was that had stirred up this food insecurity and comfort-eating had yet to hit me. All I knew was this boy could eat, and he grew fast!

In April, just in time for Joshua's sixth birthday, he and my grandmother traveled to Houston. Joshua wiggled with excitement to see a pool in our backyard. He'd been in the house for mere moments before screaming, "I want to swim! I want to swim!" Nothing could keep him from jumping in and out, and he was a regular fish in water. After our busy lives and work, it was refreshing for Eric and me to be around his energy and his innocence. For all we knew, Joshua had been living a perfectly normal and happy life after the events years ago.

Unfortunately, all that splashing in the pool gave him a painful ear infection the next day, requiring a visit to a pediatrician.

On the phone with Tanya, I explained the news. "We're going to have to postpone their flight back."

Right then and there, my sister said fateful words. "Okay, well, I don't want him."

Simple as that. *I don't want him.* I needed to check the reality of this. "What do you mean you don't want him?"

"Do *you* want him?" She answered with the biggest question of my life.

It took me a good thirty seconds to digest what she'd said. Static on the phone, Tanya clearing her throat emotionlessly, everything suddenly sounded louder. I couldn't believe it had gotten to this point. I couldn't tell whether our grandmother, at her age, could even watch him all the time. And I couldn't tell whether Tanya just didn't care.

Did I want him? The answer was yes. But for how long? A few days? A month? Forever.

From our childhood, I always looked out for Tanya. She knew I would not forsake a family member. Tanya knew how much I loved Joshua and that I would never allow him to end up in the system. She may have been taking advantage of where I stood in my life financially, but it was likely a combination of desperation and fear.

Things with Josh had ended, I'm not sure exactly when, and Tanya had married a man named Lenny and had another baby by this time. Her new husband didn't take kindly to Joshua and the trouble he caused. Immediately, thrown back twenty years in time, I knew I needed to step in again like I had the afternoon our mother walked away. Full of emotion, trauma, and sensing a call to arms, I had to take care of the situation and didn't even bother to ask what Josh's role was in being a father. I only thought of Joshua, whom neither of his parents wanted.

Finally, I told her sternly, "Tanya, this isn't a decision I can make over the phone. Eric and I need to talk about this."

Not only did Eric and I have to work through it, but we also had to see it from Grandma's perspective—a woman who had just lost her husband. She still loved and enjoyed the fulfillment of having a six-year-old around, but for how long? Eric and I still reeled from our infertility issues. Starting our own family was not happening but starting a non-traditional family and fostering my nephew posed a big, bold question mark. The rest of that spring and summer, Eric and I asked each other and ourselves, "Can we do this? *How* do we do this?"

❋❋❋

SEVEN

THE EXCHANGE

"Hell is truth seen too late."

—*Thomas Hobbes*

The drive from Texas to Pennsylvania seemed to drag on. While Eric drove the Ford Explorer, I watched the landscape begin to thicken with green and the Texas heat in August caused the road ahead to smudge with black and silver mirages. It was near Labor Day and still scalding hot. I rubbed the sweat off my thighs as I readjusted myself on the passenger's side. Towns and trees blurred as I gazed out the window. All I could do was to check the time over and over. "Five more hours, four, three…"

We sat in the car, each in different trains of thought. I was anxious and excited to become a mother to Joshua. Eric, on the other hand, had never been around little kids. He felt overwhelmed with the idea of one suddenly being in our home, and still felt lost from our inability to get pregnant. A part of me knew we had some painful issues ahead, trying to fit into the roles of mom and dad in the blink of an eye. Eric would become a father in less than a day, and I could feel the dense, gut-twisting tension in the car. Eric loved me, though, and wanted to make me happy. The two of us sat in this emotional tempest quietly, eyes on the road, as the hours rolled by.

Flying would have saved us stress, but it was important to bring along some of the things Joshua would want. I unfolded a list from my purse and noted the items I'd asked Tanya to pack: special blankets, toys, or anything else that would make the transition to his new home a little easier.

Nothing could have prepared any of us for this new life. Joshua's visit to Houston with hours of playing and fun were like little honeymoon phases. But as we drew closer to Pennsylvania, I knew this was the real deal. We were one step closer to being Joshua's parents, and on the worst of terms.

Sure, we'd made a physical check list of what we needed to house and care for a child: a room of his own, a nice bed, some toys, school clothes, and new shoes. The physical check list of parenting—at any stage in a child's development—is always easy. Talk to any foster parents. Providing the basics, home necessities, and a safe environment usually comprises the least worries. Creating a mental, emotional, and psychological checklist for what's yet to come is the biggest part. This includes therapy (what type? Which of us will need it and why?), marriage counseling (is this marriage ready for a child that's not ours?), and legal help (will we be able to adopt him?). These questions swirled around in my head, but I still had no idea the extent of damage done to Joshua. All I knew was I wanted Eric to drive faster than sixty miles per hour to get us to Pennsylvania.

I held my head in my hand and tried to think even faster about the why, what, where, and when of Joshua's abuse. The guilt of "should have" all those years ago knotted my stomach. What would have happened if Tanya had given him to me as a baby? Would much of his trauma have been prevented?

When faced with such a decision, rehoming a child, you don't think of half of the logical questions. You don't realize the magnitude of damage control after. My instinct was to get him safely home. I wanted him *out* of there. I didn't care how, or on what terms, or what we faced ahead.

But first, we had to figure out where in the world Tanya and Joshua lived. I realized after hours in the car, our directive must be to go straight into their area and figure this out ourselves. Whether we had to look it up in the Yellow Pages, call a relative, or speak to Tanya on the phone again (the thought of which made me alternately squirm or grow hot with anger), someone would point us in the right direction.

After many moves, they had finally settled into a two-story, cobbled-together rental house the next town over from where we grew up. We practically drove through people's yards in our hurry to get there, but once on their street, Eric slowed the car. We squinted to spy the address number. We could barely see the house but couldn't miss it—practically a ghost of a home. Bare, white, shabby, it crouched on the weedy lawn. It didn't have a single toy or plaything on it. We parked in the drive and Eric rearranged the car to make room for Joshua's things.

As I mounted the steps, I exhaled to relieve tension and heard the murmur of the TV from inside.

Tanya opened the door without so much as a hello. Her lips formed a tight line, holding back any kind of greeting. Behind her I could see the unkempt house. It seemed almost like a movie set: toys and trash scattered on the floor, dirty dishes anywhere but in the sink. *How is this possible?* Every mother knows what it's like to have a slovenly house at times, but this was beyond. Clearly no one had taken out the garbage in weeks. I couldn't tell if Tanya's narrow, tense eyes were due to assuming I judged her, or suspicion of our motives. Anxious to get Joshua out, I made the first move.

"Where's Joshua?" I asked, looking over her shoulder.

"He's upstairs," she finally responded. She tried to seem nonchalant about the situation, but I could tell her voice had a tinge of anxiety.

Regardless of how I paint my sister here, I know she never imagined her life—or Joshua's—to be this way. Tanya likely felt she had no choice but to give him up. And she might be happier and a little less stressed without her son.

"Do you want me to go and get him?" My words came out as nothing short of robotic. I swallowed the anger I felt that this woman was my sister, someone I had cared so much about. I made it my directive to move past these emotions, past her.

"Yeah," She answered coolly.

Up the wooden stairs, some of them littered with trash, I glanced into all the bedrooms. Joshua was not in any of them. Then I heard his footsteps above my head, running back and forth, back and forth. I walked up the stairs to the attic, the footsteps growing louder.

Dear God. With a great deal of urgency I tugged on the door. It hadn't taken me long to figure out this little boy was inside, and they had kept him trapped in the attic, tying the door shut with a rope.

It had gotten to the point that they could no longer control Joshua's behavior. Their best plan of disciplinary action was to lock this little boy in a room by himself.

On the floor a mattress, dirty plates, rotting food, and cups sat in a heap. Tears filled my eyes. I wondered how many hours he had been here. How many hours since someone had changed his clothes, bathed him, or cared for him at all. When was the last time someone had read him a bedtime story? When was the last time he ran free in the yard, or rode his bike in the park? All these thoughts, mixed with anger, filled my head and heart as I heard his little footsteps running back and forth.

I opened the door. Joshua stopped dead in his tracks. He looked stunned, as though he couldn't believe Aunt Rhonda was really here. Then he came to life. He tumbled over himself, leaping to hug me. I picked him up. I knew with everything in me that this child would never have to live in this room again. Both of us could feel the silent, sudden change. I knew I was becoming his mother at that moment. In a way, he did too. Eyes wide, hair tussled, he looked at me in a hopeful, longing way that meant, "She's here to pick me up."

I took him downstairs. I don't even remember if Tanya saw us leave the house. She might have been watching from the window with a cigarette hanging from her mouth, or equally, up in her room crying. I wouldn't have wanted to look at her face anyway. Her emotional reaction didn't matter to me. Eric loaded the car with a bag of Joshua's clothes and his bike, some of his only possessions.

"I think we have everything, Rhonda," he said solemnly.

And we certainly had everything, absolutely *every*thing this child needed or wanted. What help he would need, what problems were yet to come, we had no idea.

Buckling Joshua in the back seat, I adjusted the strap and touched his chin. He smiled and folded his hands in his lap. The feeling of finally having him safe, in our care, lifted the weight from my shoulders. This part was over.

A neighbor lady walked over before we drove away and asked quietly if we were taking him.

"Yes," I said, clearing my throat. The urge to cry was strong.

"Thank God!" the woman exclaimed. "Now I don't have to worry about him hanging out the window."

"What do you mean?" I asked.

"I guess he's never outside," she pointed to the top of the house, "so he just sits on the attic windowsill. I'm always worried something will happen to him."

The image of Joshua sitting on a windowsill three stories up sent a shock through me. I got into the passenger seat. I didn't look up at the house. I didn't care if Tanya had one last word to say (and what, honestly, could she say to us now?).

He is finally leaving this place. I'm leaving you now too, Tanya. That was the moment I cut the emotional tethers for my little sister—the one I rocked in her crib, the one I wanted to protect so badly, the one I set on Sugar Babe, and who I'd hoped to God would have good memories in this life. We drove out silently and moved toward a new life.

***

EIGHT

ROUGH START

"Beginning is easy—continuing is harder."

—*Proverb*

Fostering any child, you're warned about the nasty words the child might say: *You're not my mom!* Or *I hate living here!* What they don't tell you about is the screams. For Joshua, these were not behavioral or tantrum screams, they were psychological, blood-curdling, epic screams, stemming from the trauma—mostly during the middle of the night. I'd be jolted awake and hear the banging first. His fists beating on the bedroom door, he then gave out those shrieking, high-pitched cries. This was every night for weeks. It was months of ongoing therapy before every night became a few nights a week, and then a drip. But at the start, we were in the wild thick of it.

"The wolves…" He broke down sobbing for the third time that week. "The wolves are going to kill me."

We tried a different routine every night to see if it made a difference. Like most six-year-olds, he often didn't want to go to bed, and it would take an hour or so with me sitting beside him before he would fall asleep. I let him splash in the tub, gobble down a snack, or turn the pages of a book I read. I rubbed his forehead, like I had when he was a baby, and I held his hands. I would reassure him, "You're safe, and no wolves and no one is going to hurt you." This took a lot of time and energy every day, but I'd heave a thick sigh of exhaustion and keep on.

We also had a school pick-up and drop-off routine. Joshua was having a difficult time concentrating in his new school due to lack of sleep. He slumped out of bed every morning with dark, puffy circles under his eyes. Like any mother's, my heart broke over this.

That was it: Mother. All those years wanting to become one, and my role came in the blink of an eye. Mother. It took on a new meaning entirely. Both day and night, I worked as a nurse—a 24-hour shift, no breaks. Anyone will tell you that's motherhood at the core: tiring, exhausting, but rewarding. Becoming a mother to a child with severe mental health issues and burgeoning behavioral issues at the drop of a hat, however, doesn't give you a learning period. You jump in and survive with them. Eric, too, suddenly took the role of father, overseeing the drama, offering help but often leaving the room puzzled. These roles, I figured, would take some time getting used to.

Above all, Joshua was suddenly a son, our child, and altogether wanted by two parents. Imagine suddenly becoming loved, cared for, and spoken to like a human being after many years of neglect. Many times, I wondered if Joshua wanted to test our love through his flaring, hot tantrums. Children who come from abusive and/or traumatic backgrounds often do this—test their new parents by acting out, hitting, screaming, breaking things around the house, and testing what breaking of boundaries will make them get rejected again. This cycle often repeats itself in foster care children: new home, new violence and tantrums, and new home again. Joshua wanted to make sure he was not going to be given away again. The "wolves," however, seemed to be a different psychosis—a deep-seated fear of where he was in life. Preyed upon, hurt, and constantly threatened, that's what I imagined and knew abuse/sexual abuse felt like.

Wolves were on his mind for weeks, then months. These visions and night terrors plagued Joshua, scared us, and didn't create an environment for any rest for nearly the entire first year. Hours passed every night trying to get him to close his eyes. Did he think if he opened them, we'd be gone? It was like a game of peek-a-boo with a baby but now with a six-year-old child incredibly insecure about love, about his place with us, and whether we would stay with him. By day, it was a game of survival from the night before. The piercing screams seemed to carve out my skull, leaving room for no other thoughts than coffee, work, and starting the day over again.

That is exactly how I describe the first year being his parent: *no sleep*. For many parents, that's the newborn and sleep regression phase, but for us it was deeper, more emotionally draining, and it centered around Joshua's past.

When you're taking care of a child with mental health issues and an abusive past, you're in the thick of decisions constantly. "Should we? Can we?" But on the other hand, your mind goes blank. You unconsciously repeat patterns or do whatever will work at the time.

For us it meant our nighttime routine would go on and on, leaving Eric and I drained, without a word to say to each other during the screams. These wolves would follow Joshua. They followed all of us. Within a month, we had placed him with a child psychologist.

Freshly settled in Houston, Joshua was also very difficult to place in school. He essentially had *no* school records. Every time he'd had a behavior issue in the past, Tanya withdrew him and enrolled him in another school. His life had no educational foundation or routine. At that point, Joshua had attended kindergarten and first grade in eleven different schools. His way of life had been nomadic, moving from town to town, one school district to the next. But somehow, one teacher had leveled him up a grade even though he could not read so much as *one* word.

Academically, Joshua was a few levels down. Socially, he had a one-up at first. His first day of school revolved around being the new kid in town. Wanting badly to be liked and accepted, Joshua knew how to tell extravagant stories (some lies) that made his life seem interesting. He quickly made a pack of friends even though he was very different than the likes of his classmates. He was a wild-eyed country boy from Pennsylvania with a colorful imagination and a dark history.

At school, he took on the role of a storytelling, squirrelly little boy. Joshua loved to grab others' imaginations. He knew exactly what to do to make friends at this age—just be as loud and proud as possible.

Children can be naturally courageous at this age and often have no inhibitions. This described Joshua. When it came to answering questions, writing, or participating in school though, a clear divide came in. I imagined the teacher seeing him at his desk, stumped. He'd be chewing on a pencil, suddenly going from a bright, vibrant kid to a blank stare.

After a full evaluation, we found out that although Joshua could recite his ABCs and count to ten, he could not recognize a single word in a book. No one at home, of course, had ever read to him. Essentially, we were starting from scratch, and it was a full-time job to get Joshua up to some semblance of normal living. We knew we could keep him clothed, safe, fed, loved, and listened to, but achieving normalcy would never be a part of the agenda. We had to make up for years of lost time.

I tried to imagine what Joshua's nighttime routine looked like before he came to us, and I thought the worst: once the sun went down and the sky turned black, was he shut up in the attic? Was the door tied every night? Did anyone ever kiss him goodnight? Some aspect of his screams began to make sense—he was not used to any of this attention, while at the same time he craved more desperately. All he was given was medication to lessen his symptoms, keep him quiet, and more or less shut him down. Joshua had been on some kind of pill or another since the age of four, but he'd never had any kind of in-person therapy.

Not only Joshua, but all of us needed a psychologist. Eric, Joshua, and I had private sessions, and then we'd group together as a family. Over time and through talk and play therapy, the therapist tried to guide him toward the root of these episodes, what these "wolves" were, but Joshua, like any young child with PTSD, could not articulate those answers. Joshua had buried these memories of abuse so deeply that getting them out in the open was like hoping to find a diamond in the wrong kind of cave. They would never resurface.

He expressed his anger and "hatred" toward people who hurt him, however, such as Tanya. He wondered, "Why didn't she want me?"

Children don't forget a parent walking out on them or giving them away. I didn't forget, and Joshua didn't forget. It's a stigma carried throughout life. It eats away at how children experience love or acceptance from others. They can develop either an unhealthy dependency on other people for their security or cause them to distrust everyone. In Joshua's case, it was both. He wanted all the love and attention he could get but didn't trust it. He craved any attention, negative or positive. Yet he could find it difficult to accept our attention and seemed uncomfortable if we held his hand or kissed him goodnight.

Many children from abusive backgrounds don't know what it is to feel confident that someone will protect them—or to experience the stability which comes from that confidence. As a result, they often create make-believe worlds to cope.

Joshua enjoyed play therapy, but often confused reality with the world he created. This made getting to the truth very hard for the psychologist and for us. Oftentimes, he would reel out a long, winding story with no ending. It proved difficult for us—and even a trained psychotherapist—to pick apart. The tropes he used, certain words, feelings, anything distinguishable as a link to his abuse, felt like a game, a riddle, a constant labyrinth.

On the surface, he appeared to be a normal child blossoming with intellect and imagination.

Children make up stories about monsters, dragons, and villains all the time—especially when they are beginning to understand morality. Right and wrong concepts begin to be understood at this stage. As toddlers, they begin to figure out that doing bad things leads to harm— touching the oven, grabbing sharp objects, and the like. Around six or seven, they begin to see outside of their self-involved view to how actions have consequences morally. *If I take this package of cookies, Mom will find out. Would she know if I took just one?* Children begin to balance what they can and can't get away with, and what they should and should not do. With Joshua or other children who have mental health issues and abusive backgrounds it can be difficult to determine what approach will work best when trying to instill morals, teach about consequences, or impart basic safety rules.

One morning as I made his bed, I felt cold metal under his pillow. I pulled up the handle of a butcher knife, and my stomach dropped. I found another knife and another, of various sizes. Eric and I gathered all the kitchen knives and hid them. We waited until our next therapy appointment to talk about the knives. According to Joshua, he wanted to protect us and himself. I didn't know whether to be scared for him, of him, or simply try to love the fear away from him.

Every parent usually goes through the baby-proofing stage: safety-locking cabinet doors, putting up gates, or installing cameras. You don't expect, however, to do a sweep of your home for sharp objects your child might be hiding. Eric and I were not only terrified and in shock as the two of us scoured the kitchen for knives, skewers, or anything jagged. And further, in the garage, for tools, screwdrivers, anything usable and dangerous. We seethed with anger about why this had to happen, why any parent should be in this position, and what Joshua had experienced to cause this whirlwind of a situation to begin with. Our questions increased in both quantity and complication. "Are you going to hurt yourself? Do you plan on hurting someone else? What are these wolves you're up against?" We wondered whether we could help him find his way out of his blurred reality. What we did know is the screams never seemed to stop.

***

NINE

RED ALERT

"Just as a snake sheds its skin,
we must shed our past over and over again."

—*Buddha*

"Time heals all wounds." Not necessarily a truism. Time may help you understand where the wounds came from, why, and what you can do to prevent more. In the case of parenting a child with past trauma and mental health issues, it is not time that heals. It's *hope, love,* and *patience* that will get you through the worst days. On our worst day, Eric and I got a surprising knock on the door from Child Protective Services.

The sight of those uniforms, clipboards, and clip pens would haunt me forever. I knew these strangers would be ready to write down anything wrong in our home. I swallowed and listened to their short speech about the inspections to come. Eric stood behind me, white as a ghost. Suddenly *we* were the spectacle, the ones on display, after having tried so hard to do everything we possibly could for Joshua. I nodded, complied, or softly answered "yes" or "no" to their initial questions. I felt I faced a firing squad.

With Child Protective Services or anyone in authority, you can't struggle or fight in that moment. What you'd like to say goes out the window: "But I'm a good parent." "We're taking the best care of him." Even if you know the truth, you still have to let these strangers see for themselves.

We desperately wanted to know *why* they had come. The answer could be followed back to something Joshua had said to a teacher, who then sounded the red alert.

Before the moment we opened the door to these officials, we tackled Joshua's instability anyway we could. We'd made use of the learning disability resources at school, taken him to doctor appointments, after-school activities like soccer, and increasingly, therapy sessions. At this point, we were each in the chair once a week. My first thoughts often came out at the negative end of the spectrum: *There is no way all three of us are going to survive and come out on the other side of this. How are we going to get out without losing a limb or our minds first?* A few years had gone by and landed us in some psychologically rough terrain.

During his first years with us, Joshua had a habit of urinating anywhere but in the toilet—and most definitely everywhere in his bedroom. It started in the closet. I could smell something acrid and sour but never found the source since he would move clothes out of the way and pee toward the back of the closet, all over the wall. This escalated to urinating all over the bedroom, to the point where we had to pull up the carpet, tack strips and all. It was completely soaked through.

He had a problem with bed-wetting, necessitating Pull-Ups at night. This issue was front and center in our therapy sessions. It is common for children who experience sexual abuse to have problems with bed-wetting. Stress, anxiety, PTSD, sleep disorders, or any form of physical or psychological distress are the root cause for nocturnal enuresis, or bedwetting. That's something I knew from my time nursing. But I never expected it to be continuous. Day and night, it felt like one long potty-training session. There was never a time we could forget it and relax.

Just as it had been years before, Joshua's loss of bowel control was a huge red flag. He was in the middle grades and it appeared patterns repeated as if by muscle memory. The issue might be directly related to him wanting autonomy over his own body and actions. Peeing on the floor can be as unconscious as sleepwalking, but this was a conscious, almost calculated effort.

I tried to pry apart the psychosomatic reasons. Did he just not *want* to make it to the bathroom? Was it laziness? Did he figure it wouldn't matter because we were just going to clean it up? Did he know this took our effort and attention away from him?

Honestly, we had no idea. It could have been one of any number of things our psychologist suggested. It was again in the realm of stress and anxiety or assertion of bodily control. Sometimes, there was no room even to think about it—only to sigh, clean up, instruct him on what he should be doing and why ("because that's what we all do"). And the cycle would repeat until the house smelled like we owned ten dogs instead of our two! One thing we did know is that Joshua wasn't too shy about telling people the state of our home.

Going back to the day Child Protective Services was called: Joshua had told one of his teachers we were abusing him, beating him with a belt, and making him sleep on a concrete floor!

We had yet to replace the old carpet, and this is what landed us in the laser beam of suspicion.

Of course, redoing the floor was on our master to-do list, but with everything else going on, the installation wasn't going to happen in a single day.

What happened next was a rumor mill from teacher to administration to Child Protective Services. Coming home from school one Friday, Joshua related the seemingly normal events of the day.

"...some guy took pictures of me at school today," he said matter-of-factly, like it had been just another day.

Closing the fridge door, I turned around. "What are you talking about, Joshua?"

"Yeah, he asked me to take my clothes off," he answered, shrugging.

Of course, my knees began to knock. I felt the sore grip of panic in my chest as the questions rolled off my tongue. "What? What are you talking about?"

"Well, I was in my underwear, and he took some pictures of me."

In under a minute I was on the phone trying to reach the school. After hours, the answering machine popped on, and my mind raced as to what to do next. Any good parent's instinct on hearing the words "underwear" and a stranger "taking pictures" is going to be set to code red. You don't know what to think at that moment other than that your child (1.) had been with a predator or (2.) had gotten a medical examination of some kind without parental permission.

Sitting in my kitchen, head in my hands, I hoped to God it was the second. I knew cases like this from hearing about and seeing them as a pediatric nurse, so I did think about the possibilities with Child Protective Services. Honestly, considering Joshua's dramatically colorful style of speaking, this was probably bound to happen.

Some things Joshua said I knew came from pure imagination, storytelling, trying to get a rise, but this was too site-specific and curt. He said it nearly without any exaggeration at all. The next day—the worst day of our lives yet—we got the knock on the door. After everything Joshua had endured from his parents, *we* were the ones getting investigated for child abuse and neglect. Eric and I looked at each other knowingly. *Here we go.*

This became a tipping point for us as individuals and as a married couple. Not only had we invested every drop of energy, time, and money into Joshua's wellbeing, but my whole career was centered around pediatric health. A woman who works a high-level position at a pediatric hospital getting investigated for child abuse? It already looked like a nightmare of a newspaper headline, and an attack on who I was at my core: a nurse, a nurturer!

Thankfully, this situation dissolved. It also explained the photographs Joshua said had been taken of him at school. After questioning all of us in separate rooms and taking pictures of the house, they left, stating that we would hear back from the Child Protective Services office early the following week.

The weekend was excruciatingly tense, but we tried not to be punitive to Joshua. We walked around each other like ghosts—speechless, blank, and at least on my part, shell-shocked. At Sunday dinner, I set plates out and had Joshua take a seat. Somehow, I was able to summon calmness, peace, and forgiveness. I cleared my throat and asked him what we wanted to know: *why* would he give anyone the impression he was being abused or neglected, when we opened our home to him in pure love?

He looked at me with sweet, innocent eyes and said, "I thought they would take me away and I would live with someone else for a while."

"Why, Joshua?" I asked, tearfully. "Why would you want to live with someone else?"

He went on to tell us he didn't really want to live with anyone else, but he thought it was normal to go live with someone else when he got in trouble or needed discipline. Joshua was still under the impression he was only loved when on his best behavior, only seen if rowdy, and only heard if he acted out. The "wolves" could have been an embodiment of his fears, dark history, former abusers, yes, but could also have been an inner voice screaming to be heard, noticed, and justified. Did he feel like the wolf? The bad little wolf who no one could tame and so was left to fend for himself?

I thought of the book *Where the Wild Things Are* and imagined a young boy in a wolf costume, or a child who believed he should be treated like a monster for no reason. Underneath the teeth and the scary features, he was still just a wild little boy. Even during the worst of our days, we knew Joshua was only a child under the memories we couldn't unlock. His innocence, an entire bulk of his childhood, had been stripped away. Was the wolf really *him*? Was he afraid of himself?

Either way, we knew some demons had been unleashed the moment Child Protective Services charged through our home. We could never undo this kind of intrusion or invasion of our privacy, let alone recover our trust in what Joshua might or might not say. Although it never cost me my job or social standing, it permanently affected what I feared could happen. The phrases "the past is the past" or "water under the bridge" are just about as handy as saying abuse or trauma doesn't affect you long-term. Nothing could compare with these two events, and it's not something you easily forget or forgive, as much as you love your child.

Time would never heal the humiliation and tumult of what had just happened. Still, we knew Joshua was only a child—capable of saying the first thing on his mind, despite the context. Our emotions remained. Eric started to feel detached and distant. Joshua ping-ponged back and forth between normal, hyper, quiet, and at times, a tornado of anger. I tried to sit silent when all I wanted to do was scream.

❖❖❖

TEN

HANGING ON HOPE

"One lie is enough to question all truths."

—*Anonymous*

There are times in some marriages when the two start to see each other less. Work life, kids, chores, and daily demands are common dividing factors.

What once bound us together—wanting a family so badly, to start a life, and then to take care of Joshua together—slowly became the factor breaking us apart. Granted, this wasn't a typical way of starting a family and becoming parents. Our marriage became entangled in survival— simply getting through each day alive. We clung to hope wherever we could find it. That is how I describe this period of our lives.

Infidelity, or at least temptation, may test many relationships. A stranger catches your eyes and draws you away from monotony. Suddenly, the flame grows, and you feel wanted, spoken to, or heard in ways the relationship doesn't merit. Sometimes it's just a glance or a conversation. Sometimes a full-blown affair. Either way, cheating usually is an offshoot of something lacking in the relationship or that needs repair.

In our case, I began to notice the signs in Eric. Distant, quieter than usual, going in and out of the house in a hurry—these are usually what spouses begin to do in a double life.

The first proof of Eric's indiscretion was in an email I found. We shared a computer, and I'd begun researching online classes for my bachelor's degree. I logged in and Eric's email opened. I noticed an email from a woman thanking him. I remembered feeling so many emotions. The woman described the meeting for coffee and my heart sank. More and more, I noticed Eric kept his cell phone out of reach. When I asked him about this his only explanation was "she was a friend." Little did I know this would not be the last of these "friends."

Several months later another email surfaced and this time it was a woman sharing how much she cared for Eric. I recognized the name as someone who worked in his industry. I felt like I was breaking in two. I couldn't save Joshua and now the possibility of not saving my marriage crippled me. Eric was out of town when I found this email and although I knew where he was, I didn't know what hotel he was staying in. I found myself on the phone calling every hotel and on the third call found him. I told him, "Either come home immediately and address this, or you will find your bags packed."

The next day, he came home. We began concentrating our therapy sessions on saving our marriage. Eric isn't someone who freely talks about his feelings, so therapy was an uphill battle. I did not understand and didn't see what was right in front of me. I still thought I could save everyone and everything.

About three months later while paying the bills I noticed a reappearing number on Eric's cell phone bill. The number appeared every day about the same time—every morning right after Eric would leave the house and right before he came home.

One morning at the kitchen table, I heard a buzz from his coat pocket. Slipping my hand in, I pulled out the screen to see a number with a local area code and no name. It was a friendly message; along the lines of "What are you doing?" None of his male friends would have asked such a simple, airy question. Surely, a friend would know Eric was at home this early.

That's the moment I knew. My husband would continue finding other ways for fulfillment. Even if I wanted to scream "do it again and you're gone" or give him the final ultimatum, I knew it *would* happen again. I began to question, *Is this something he can stop? Has this become a coping mechanism or addiction—to have a second life away from ours because ours has proved too painful?*

Our home went into a downward spiral of parenting, disagreeing, his distance, my tears, Joshua's screaming, and none of us could control it. I couldn't control my inner anger. Eric couldn't control his habits. I knew my husband hadn't expected this from his life, or to be put in the position of Joshua coming between he and his wife. He'd had a cushy, well-adjusted childhood with stability and structure. It was hard for him to connect with Joshua's hardships, and what he'd gone through. Instability, poverty, abandonment, and trauma were things I knew even if I felt overwrought with anger—anger for Joshua's past, and anger that I couldn't control the present, or the future. Naturally, I leaned toward empathy for Joshua's behavior, whereas Eric veered toward confusion. At times, he lashed out even when he didn't mean to.

"This is how you act at the table, at the restaurant." Eric would stamp his words down and try to discipline him the best he could. "Why don't you do that?"

Why Joshua didn't always absorb what most normal children do—how to listen or take in lessons or discipline—boggled Eric. He had a difficult time understanding how this boy's brain functioned. The more Eric tried the more Joshua drew back and tested the boundaries. I knew my husband came close to giving up altogether. That's when he found himself drawn away almost magnetically. Most affairs begin under that pressure. Meeting another person can be an easy distraction, a nice little tangent from the hardships of marriage and parenthood.

It wasn't a physical affair with anyone that I'm aware of, but indiscretions followed. Whether through his industry or at the gym, he always seemed able to meet women. First, it was an email, then a text here and there, a conversation, then a string of interactions and daily "good mornings" that seemed a little more than what friends do. This ended face-to-face at coffee shops. There were text messages with phrases like "Good morning sexy," things I thought he only said to me.

Crushed, that's the exact sentiment from any betrayed spouse. It's a nasty feeling of "Why? Why me?" I realized we had lived in utter decay all those years. Surviving day to day as parents didn't give us much time alone, and no one was going to step up and tell us, "Go on dates. Spend time alone. Get more therapy and see what went wrong." There would never be a sane voice telling us to work on our marriage. Lying in bed, looking at the empty space where Eric usually slept, I tried to backtrack to what we could have done right. Life had begun to crumble around me. I found some truth in deep thought: *I'm so angry. Am I an angry wife?*

Most days, even if I kept a calm and collected temperament, I still seethed with anger. Living with me behind closed doors, in the intimacy of a bedroom, was no easy task. Trying to be soft, loving, and gentle to Joshua—even during times of hurricane emotions, chaos, and fear—often led me to boiling inside, bottling up my feelings, or becoming rigid—even toward Eric. *Is that why he wanted to find warmth in someone else? Was I turning into a different person?*

These are painful questions for the betrayed spouse to ask themselves, but always best served with humility. Yes, it was wrong for my husband to break our marriage vows, though I began to see I needed to change my behavior too. In that, I saw hope.

The root of our marriage was not rotten. Throughout all of this, Eric and I did have a foundation of love, but the situation with Joshua felt hopeless. Reaching out to other women was his way of hanging on. He could be of help by listening to others in a vulnerable situation. He wanted to help counteract the downhill battle at home. It seemed he was thinking, *If I'm no good at home, I'm no good to either of them. If Rhonda is closer to Joshua, and Joshua is closer to Rhonda, then what is my identity in this relationship?*

Whenever he strayed—and it happened multiple times—I would find out and confront Eric. An altercation would follow. Some were worse than others. Occasionally, women's messages seemed benign and innocent while others described the bar where they would meet for a glass of wine. Once I heard a message a woman had left him about meeting up during a business trip and she hoping he hadn't brought me with him.

Slowly, I started to become a different woman—suspicious, uneasy, frustrated, and even angrier than before, twenty-four hours a day. I wanted to change my behavior, but did he?

As a wife, I had to keep my husband in check. As a nurse, a *pediatric* nurse no less, I had no control over Joshua. I could not fully help him even if I had phenomenal resources and a close proximity to one of the best children's hospitals in the country. Even *they* couldn't help. This created in me feelings of helplessness and lack of hope, but still I hung on.

With all the stress, migraines attacked more often. One evening, I doubled over in pain, barely able to make it to the shower to steam off the pounding in my head.

Even with migraine medication, I experienced breakthrough headaches. My doctor gave me Vicodin for these. I soon discovered that these little white pills helped me escape reality the same as Eric escaped his but with less of a moral quandary. After all, it was a prescription. I took them every day when I got home from work. I popped one or two and went about my evening in a haze.

For the next several months, drug dependence kept the pain away and became my new reason to make it through each day. While driving home one evening I looked around at a blurry, unfamiliar road, way off the mark from our neighborhood. *Where am I and how did I get here?* My hands barely had a grip on the steering wheel, and I squinted through green and black colors—the grass and the asphalt. That was the wake-up call. What was truly worth getting to this point?

I veered off the road and put the car into park. I tried to think back through the last few months—the emails, fights, and hours in counseling. The screaming, the wolves…and then, the feeling of nothingness. My head floated in numbness. Hurting myself or worse, someone else, seemed to be the trajectory I was on here. If I stopped taking the drug, I would let the pain come back into my system—the lies, the hurt, and my lack of control. Sometimes, confronting the pain starts a new mode of healing. You let your body get stronger. You push through to what matters most. You hang onto hope, even if it's by a single finger.

***

ELEVEN

PLAYING WITH FIRE

*"What matters most is
how you walk through the fire."*

—*Charles Bukowski*

It was a typical day at work until I received a frantic call from Eric at home. He described the situation as a "small fire in the garage." A sharp, suffocating scent had alerted him. He called 911 first and next, my cell phone. Eric told me his suspicions. All signs pointed to Joshua, which set off an alarm in me to rush home. I opened the door to a billow of smoke that rolled through the house. We'd caught him playing with matches many times, lighting and blowing them out. But this time he'd balled them up inside paper and kindled a disaster.

Even though the fire had smoldered out by the time Eric called the fire department, the smoke had entered the air conditioner vents. Everything in the garage was lost, including a great deal of our patience. Flooring had to be replaced and walls painted. This added another crowning moment to all my anger and frustration. Eric and I were being torn further and further apart emotionally and as parents.

In the midst of all this, the phone rang out of the blue. Tanya wanted to know how Joshua was doing. *How? How is he doing? We're in the trenches!* I wanted to scream, then hung up. I am not sure what I meant by we: "We are done," but I'd said it. "We're fine, fine, and we're done."

On her own, Tanya decided she would make the trip to Houston and take Joshua. At the time, all I had was the power of attorney. So when she showed up in my driveway and knocked on my door, nothing could stop her from taking him. Even if I wanted to scream, throw in the towel, or run away, I didn't want to give up Joshua. Being "done" didn't mean abandoning him. Being done meant we needed help mentally and emotionally. But the last thing we needed was help from the woman who'd begun this hellfire of neglect and the robbery of his childhood, the years we tried desperately to make up for. The expression in Tanya's eyes made her look cold and driven, soulless.

"What are you doing here?" I asked her, looking at the tall figure lingering behind her in the driveway. A man she called her "pastor"—from a small church back in Pennsylvania—had driven with her.

"Obviously he's not doing well." She said. "I want him back." She nodded her head toward the pastor's pick-up truck.

I loved Joshua. As much as we'd been through, we had cried, screamed, and grown together. He was *my* son. *Our* son. Right there in the doorway, Tanya called to Joshua and gave him the ultimatum: "I want you to tell me right now. Do you want to stay with Rhonda, or do you want to come with your mother?"

For a long time, Joshua had never heard the word "mother" in regard to Tanya, but still the word had impact for him. Every child desires to be with their mom regardless of how they've been treated. It's an unconscious pact. The mother-child dynamic always proves hard to sever. In a slow, painful half hour, we packed his suitcase amid tears and awkward silence. Tanya took the handle of Joshua's luggage, and without a word, took him. She and the quiet, stiff pastor she'd brought didn't even bother to stay the night.

What they might have said to him, or what transpired in the car between the three will always haunt me. Did he throw a tantrum? Did he fight back physically? Was he close to setting something on fire? Something momentous or sinister must have happened on the road trip because once in Pennsylvania, they drove Joshua straight to the small local hospital and told them, "He's possessed. He's speaking to the devil."

Religion had never drawn Tanya—ever. We didn't know if this had come from her desperation, the man's influence over her, or if she was merely misguided. Instead of taking Joshua to a church, he wound up in a hospital psych ward. I only found out because of a voice mail from his case manager there after two days. Tanya had dropped him off, right then and there, and I had been the emergency contact. No one had a discharge plan in place. I imagined the worst—Joshua stuck in a cell, drugged, waiting innocently for someone to come get him. That night, I flew to Pennsylvania myself, and the nightmare turned out to be worse than I thought.

In the middle of the ward's rec room, I walked closer to a group of older boys, teens, and our tiny boy in a chair off to the side. His head was hung down, slobber dribbling down his chin and onto his lap—a scene you'd only see in movies, and a terrible one at that. Seeing your child appearing soulless, blank, a shadow of who he once was, will set a parent aflame. I marched over and put down my bag.

"Joshua," I said, putting a hand on his shoulder. He looked up, dead-eyed. "It's me. It's…"

Joshua was so medicated he didn't know who I was. Before I tried any further, I saw my grandmother. She had arrived right before I did. Her first instinct was to blame me.

"How could you let her take him? How did you think it would end?" Despite how we'd felt about it, I knew I had no legal recourse to keep him, or to keep Tanya from him. While Grandma stayed with Joshua in the room, I flew through the ward trying to find a nurse, a doctor, or the case manager—anyone to listen, or tell me what had happened.

I gave them the gist of the story. *She gave him to me. She came to get him. I'm here. I'm here now, and he's coming back with me—whether it's legal or not.*

The case manager told me they had found a residential treatment placement for Joshua in Erie. An indefinite amount of time, that's the answer they gave me about the length of his stay. But I wanted a plan before I left Pennsylvania. On a call with the hospital case manager and the residential center case manager, we formulated a tentative one. Joshua would be placed in a residential treatment center in Erie until a further plan could be made to get him to a treatment center in Texas.

Satisfied, I took him to be admitted in Erie, and then went back home. Five months later I flew back, wanting to check on him. Most of all, I wanted to speak with a psychiatrist who could shed some light on Joshua's progress.

It hadn't taken me long to figure out that Tanya, once again, had completely checked out and left his care to me. Worse, Joshua's mental health not only hadn't improved, but had even regressed. And all of it had been avoidable. So many years of our care for him had been undone. Home, our home, that's where Joshua *should* have stayed.

We engaged in a game of logistics and jumping through hoops with the psychology team back in Texas. That's what it would take to get him across the country to Houston. Getting him back became our new mission.

No matter what it would take, no matter how much hell we had been through or would go through, this little boy rotting in a psych ward wasn't where the story would end. Seeing him, head low, drool hanging over his lips—this image was the breaking point. If Eric and I didn't take care of him, this would be his future—sedated, silenced, not even a child anymore. How many years would that go on? I looked at his empty room, toys scattered, bedding still rumpled and unmade. I pulled up the comforter, folding it over the fitted sheet. Nothing done to our home—no fire, no damage, no mental health crisis—was worth allowing Joshua to live in that state.

For Joshua to have a discharge plan, we were required to participate in therapy sessions over the phone every week with his physician and his case manager. It would still take time. Weeks became months. After five to six months, it was finally time to bring Joshua back west. I might ask why all of this had happened, but there was no answer to that. One thing we realized, though. No matter what Joshua did, how bad his behavior got, how many fires got started, he needed us.

***

TWELVE

SPEECHLESS

"The truth hurts but silence kills."

—*Unknown*

N o words. I had no words when I saw Joshua in the treatment center in Erie on the day of his birthday. I only recall frozen images. Thin, sallow, blonde hair, sparse and falling out in patches, he was a shadow of who he'd been: the bright, high-energy boy who got into trouble. Even the idea of him getting into trouble, doing anything, feeling anything, being *alive,* tasted bitter to me. Not only was his medication out of whack, but Joshua had first stopped eating, and then speaking, altogether.

This was far from the birthday celebration I would have hoped for. When in Houston with us, Joshua loved a big, juicy spread of crawfish. So, before our flight, I had gone to his favorite restaurant and gotten some. Although the rest of the people on my flight to Pennsylvania did not appreciate the smell of an entire cooler of crawfish, I knew Joshua would. This would give him a sense of home, of that Gulf coast, southern comfort, and I wanted him to know Texas could be his forever home.

Trips to Pennsylvania were filled with excitement, fear and lots of anxiety.

It's nothing you ever expect life to throw at you: visiting a child in a psych ward far away. Outside of work, all I thought about was traveling back to him. On these trips, I would either fly into Cleveland or Pittsburgh and then drive to Erie, and I had it all mapped. Usually, I brought along something Joshua would like.

That day walking into the treatment center, I carried the cooler of crawfish with the anticipation of seeing him again. I hadn't seen Joshua for several months.

"Let me take you to him," an escort said. "He's in the playroom."

It was a wide, open room with chairs, some shelves, and toys, and a group of children sat or stood. I scanned the room. *Where is he?* I looked around for help and asked the therapist.

"He's right there," she said, pointing. Finally, the shock set in. A little boy, skeletal and with balding, frayed hair, that was Joshua. He could have been a poster child for malnourishment. The questions began to rush out, "What? How… Why didn't you let me know this was happening?"

Someone—it didn't matter who—someone said, "Well, we're trying to give him PediaSure."

That wasn't enough. "Why didn't you *tell* me though?" I snapped back.

After Joshua gave a soft, empty "Hello," he sat down at a table with me. An entire group of adults stood amazed as I opened the cooler of crawfish and Joshua pulled out each one, snapped the heads off, sucked out the meat—and ate every single one. All that was left was a greasy pool on paper towels and the wide-eyed stares of the staff. Hungry, starved, Joshua had probably just eaten his first real meal in weeks. I couldn't believe any place would allow a child to get to this point. As I said, he would literally have fit the diagnosis for severe malnutrition.

Thank God, we had finally found a place in San Antonio that would accept his Medicaid. I got permission, that day, to fly him out myself. Driving from Houston, Eric met us, and we got Joshua settled into a new plan of care, and out of that hellish scene. Slowly, we began to see glimmers of who this boy was again—jittery, talkative, always poking and prodding for a reaction or to make someone laugh. That silent ghost I saw that morning in Erie had never been Joshua.

He had always been a natural born storyteller.

Every time he told a particular story or narrative, it was for a reason. He had a strong need to be heard and more importantly, to feel important to the person listening. Joshua wanted his listener to be completely transfixed, intrigued, and even transformed by something he would say. In his words and expressions, he would grab someone's attention, and as soon as he sensed their focus, the story would become more and more intense. Sometimes, that was exactly his interest—for it to be *more,* slightly untrue, and hand crafted from his own little reality. Afterall, Joshua was a child with a childlike mind.

Stretching the truth and telling stories related back to him struggling with the feeling of not being wanted and needing to find his identity. It was important for him to feel that chemical rush of feeling wanted or needed—even if it were only for a few minutes of engaging someone in a story.

Some of the stories were much more elaborate, depending on who was listening and how he felt about the person. Sometimes there was a specific kind of attention Joshua mined for. With details, imagery, each sentence better than the next, he wanted to be admired and the center of attention. He wanted to make sure this story was something no one else had or knew—almost like an intimate secret. (He would have been a master in sales or as a lawyer!)

Once, Joshua made up a story about a ranch we owned and visited often. As he told it, there on the land, we had a creamy, white and beige longhorn named Blueberry Wine. People were drawn in and asked questions, which he gobbled up. It was a story told so well even acquaintances believed it. Living in Houston, Texas, having a ranch might be plausible. Other stories were meant only to grab a person's attention, and quickly.

He once wove a story about owning a twelve-foot-deep saltwater pool with a dolphin, which, of course, no one would believe even if we were multi-millionaires. Joshua also knew it was so absurd it would grab people's attention lightning fast in that moment, and that he had something he wanted in return—their complete attention and awe (albeit with raised eyebrows).

First a ranch, then a dolphin, and then a speedboat came into play.

That was more believable material. In his stories, he and Eric would spend the weekend together on the water. None of it true, but it was reasonable enough to have the listener's focus. *Was he being an imaginative kid, or was I enabling him to lie?* I wondered.

Looking back on the psychology and mental health aspects of what Joshua had gone through, I knew getting attention and care was important to him. This need aroused vivid, colorful stories in him. It created scenarios—and my goodness, created *fires* at one point. Everything from his stories, strengths, weaknesses, and behavioral problems had to deal with this concept of having a voice: speaking his mind. To be nothing like that quiet, half-sized, bare-boned ghost he'd been that day at the treatment center.

Storytelling gave him the one thing he thought other people had—love, attention, admiration—but on a much more simplistic level. Despite all our hurdles, I know Joshua loved Eric and me. We were "Mom and Dad," not Aunt Rhonda and Uncle Eric. But part of him still wanted his mom to love him and to want him—no matter how many times she left, abandoned, and ignored him. To tell these types of stories offered him a little fantasy-based therapy.

Some of Joshua's narratives were for short-term gains. For example, he went over to the neighbors and told this elaborate story that his great-grandmother, my grandmother, got hit and killed by a bus. He related the details that Mom had been crying, grieving, planning a funeral, and we had to fly back to Pennsylvania for a service. That's when I got a knock on the door from the neighbor, a casserole and flowers in hand. With a half-smile of sympathy, she handed me the gifts with a soft, loving gesture.

"I don't understand. What are these for?" I asked.

She told me what Joshua had said, and knowing how close I was to my grandmother, she was offering condolences.

"My grandmother wasn't killed!" I cried out. "She wasn't hit by a bus!"

A minute later I stood in Joshua's room where I demanded a much-needed explanation. The story was so specific, so emotionally drawn out, and completely random.

When I asked Joshua, "Why would you tell her that?" He replied, "Well, she made a cake, and I wanted a piece of cake."

"Joshua, why didn't you just ask for a piece of cake?" I threw my hands up in the air. It was funny, but not at the time. Lying about death to get a piece of cake was just about the sneakiest entrance into the game of storytelling and attention-getting.

"But Mom! Everybody that's in a sad situation or has a birthday, gets cake!" He yelled back and shrugged. "So, I knew she would give me a piece of that cake if she felt sad for me."

It certainly didn't make sense to me right then, but I understood that need for him, of receiving complete attention, and he was going to get it however he felt he could. For the few minutes he reeled through a story, he was his listener's center, their focal point, and he could hold all their emotions—positive or negative. It just so happened this time he was rewarded for it and got the piece of cake he wanted. Truly, he had a mouthful of deceit—sometimes cute and sweet, but other times, hurtful.

Although his storytelling never waned, his narratives became darker as he got older. The stories became more about risk, and at times it could be about someone else and could get that person into trouble. Oftentimes, the stories scared me about who Joshua might become or who he really was. Whether I wanted to accept it or not he was showing signs of a diagnosis I was fearful of acknowledging, which went beyond special needs. Something deeper, darker, and maybe even more narcissistic or sociopathic, or full of a desire to inflict pain.

This wasn't always his intention, but when driven, provoked, or drawn to do so, it's almost like Joshua subconsciously wanted to hurt someone, even a stranger—just to feel what expending hurt was like, since he himself had been so deeply hurt in his own life story. Some of these stories in his teen years were centered on someone wronging him—a tale that would usually never be true, but he would make it elaborative enough to be true. Once, I got a call from school that Joshua had told the teacher someone stole fifty dollars from him. The finger got pointed at a specific kid.

"Joshua has never and would never go to school with fifty dollars on him," I said, stunned. "He probably doesn't have that much in his piggy bank. That's just absolutely not true."

Sometimes I stood on the other side of the story—refereeing between fantasy and the truth. I was his "second voice." Sometimes, this was an arduous task, and I was on the receiving end of hurrying through an explanation. ("No, no, that is not true!") No matter what, I am glad I could be Joshua's second voice, that echo chamber to his thoughts and feelings, to explain what he couldn't about himself. From that day on, picking him up from the treatment center, I knew what Joshua needed the most—someone to rescue him, someone to look twice, and someone to truly listen.

Here I'll backtrack a few months, to when Joshua returned to live with us. After five months in the San Antonio treatment center, we began discussing his transition back home. It had been so many weekly trips back and forth from Houston to San Antonio. I remember the day the therapist asked me, "Are you ready to take him home?" I wanted to respond "of course" immediately, without hesitation. But was I, were *we* ready? I didn't know what ready really meant. Eric and I wanted to move forward, though, so after a couple of weeks of planning we brought him home. We would take another chance on Joshua.

❖❖❖

THIRTEEN

THE WONDER YEARS

"When you get to a certain age,
there is no coming back."

—*Brian Clough*

One warm, spring day, I waited outside the elementary school in the pick-up line. This was his last year before middle school, and in fifth grade, he felt like a big kid, a "tween," a preadolescent. With a beaming, wide smile, Joshua came barreling down the sidewalk and up to the car. He opened and closed the door in one swing. Slinging off his backpack, the boy clearly had something to say, and settled himself into the seat.

"Mom," he interjected into the silence. "I need you to know I'm mature."

I smiled. "What happened at school for you to make this determination, Joshua?"

"It wasn't at school, but I'm mature enough to get—" he paused an instant for effect, "a girlfriend." The cutesy nature of these words tickled me. What was once the addition of a new dog, cat, a pet, or anything he wanted on a whim as a child, had turned into his want for a female counterpart, a girlfriend.

"Why do you think you're mature enough?" I asked.

Not even bothering to whisper, or hold back, he finally said firmly,

"I have three hairs down there…"

Giving myself about five seconds to soak this in, I nodded with a grin. "Joshua, I appreciate you sharing but you really don't need to tell me every single thing going on…down there…"

Most parents would have loved this kind of transparency. Preteens usually hide, grunt over, or refuse to talk about these sorts of things. And Joshua held in so much, so much of his voice, identity, and trauma. It came as a surprise that he was clear as crystal 'when it came to all things puberty. He had no filter, and I was usually the springboard for his private discoveries. Nothing was ever too gross, too weird, or too personal to share with me. Unlike most preteens whose mouths are a steel trap, Joshua's was a floodgate.

"Oh, yes." He nodded confidently. "I've said it before. Mothers need to know."

These confessions were a weird collage of things he would share at random. When he noticed a single, dark hair under his armpit, he raced out to show me—pulling up his sleeve like it was a gift of manhood! We laugh now. Those were the cute, beginning, coming-of-age preteen years—of tumultuous emotions, of extreme highs and dirt lows. As we watched Joshua become older—around the age of twelve—despite all the new bodily changes, there was a concern about his lack of growth.

It must be all the meds he's on. Our pediatrician had possible theories on why his growth, weight, and stature wasn't back up to par even after he started eating well, gaining weight, and recovering from the hell at the treatment center. The doctor had a point. Joshua had been on medications since the age of four, which made his growth off-kilter. X-rays of his hands gave us an idea of the bone growth and plates, which didn't show signs of normal progression. We were referred to an endocrinologist, a specialist who focuses on the hormonal aspect of "Is he where he's supposed to be for his age?"

Part of that exam was to measure his testes, which they compared to a long string of beads. This was a teaching facility, and a medical fellow came in to do his examination, after which the attending physician walked in the door. Joshua stood there straight-faced and serious as you could expect. Finally, he perked up.

"Doctor, you don't need to play with me because she already has," he said nonchalantly, nodding a head towards the door and the female medical fellow.

My stomach dropped, and I jumped in. "No, no, no, Joshua. Nobody's playing with you. She did a *physical exam...*" I stressed those words so he could remember them.

Honestly, I was wrung out with fear because there I sat, the director of pediatrics at this established hospital, and he might go back to school saying, "Yeah, my mom took me to some lady, and then some guy who played with me today!"

We laugh about it now, but that's honestly what he thought they were doing. Merely "playing" was his interpretation. Going back to what happened to him in early childhood, it made sense because that's what he knew—how to detach, deconstruct, and disassociate from certain things. Either he had a way of sugarcoating it, or of going straight for the jugular. During his preteen years, Joshua would come out with these things, no holding back, and I would often think, "Why do you feel the need to tell me this?"

So many times, he repeated that phrase: "Mom, mothers need to know everything." I was worried every time Joshua would say, "Mom, I need to tell you something." I was afraid his unhealthy view of relationships and sex would be perpetuated by what he would hear at school. After consulting with the psychologist, Eric and I decided to sit down with him to determine what he knew and understood. In Joshua's mind, regardless of how old he was, or what he knew about sex, he felt it was important for me to know everything going on with him.

One morning, Eric got him up for school, and Joshua came out of his bedroom still half-asleep, bedraggled, and handed his pillow to Eric only to say, "Dad, I humped this pillow all night long. You're going to need to wash it."

Eric gave a disgusted yell. "You put that in the washer yourself!

Joshua's thought processes or his inability to have any kind of self-consciousness often led to the sentiment of "this is just normal and not embarrassing conversation—no worries, mom!" Not too many days later, after the pillow event, we took him to his regular pediatrician appointment, and he only knew it was a doctor. This kid had seen an array of specialists—fifty or sixty or more: behavioral, psychiatric, and medical—and I always tried to explain what each one was for. In the examination room, the doctor asked, "Well, Joshua how are you feeling?"

"I'm good."

"Is there anything you want to share with me?"

Oh no, here it is, I thought. *What is he going to overshare to near-strangers now?*

"I need you to help me with these explosions I'm having every day," he stated, matter-of-factly. The doctor and I exchanged wide, clueless looks.

"Well, you're gonna find out sooner or later, but I've got some sores!" He made a gesture near his lap. "I've got like a hundred explosions going on every day."

Then it clicked inside, *Oh my gosh. This child is talking about masturbating.*

The doctor and I looked at each other. It was a moment of "Who should cut in first here—parent or medical professional?"

Inching closer, the pediatrician followed through with the physical exam, and Joshua did in fact have a rash of blisters. The doctor handed him nine small KY Jelly packs, and gave him the instructions, "Now, you can't use more than two of these a day."

"Well, that's just not gonna work for me," Joshua said, holding the packs of jelly. "These explosions just won't stop."

Blushing, leaving that room in nervous giggles, I was mortified this conversation was even happening. But now I can look back and laugh. Joshua wanted to use his voice and be starkly honest and tell the doctor—point blank—what was going on. If only I'd had that kind of straightforwardness to figure out the rest! Sure, he used some strange terminology, but wanted to explain his body and his newfound discoveries, "Look at this! I'm not sure what to do with it all!" So, unlike the years we had spent digging for info—trying to get to the root of Joshua's trauma, problems, and find a solution—this part of him was completely out in the open. He was curious, downright bold, and exactly what those preteen years were—full of wonder.

***

FOURTEEN

MOOD SWINGS

*"Adolescence is a new birth, for the higher and more
completely human traits are now born."*

—G. Stanley Hall

"**M**o-o-o-o-m, I've got your dog…" Joshua said in a sing-songy, taunting voice from the balcony of our house, where he had three things: a sense of sinister power, our pet dog Cassie, and a knife. "…and I'm going to kill her."

A teenager and in the thick of hormones, that's when this event happened. His typical routine when he didn't have school was to stay up late watching TV and sleep late into the day. He would get up and stumble down to the kitchen for something to eat before returning to his bedroom to play video games or flip channels. We tried parental controls and had his television turn off at midnight, but he would then play games or listen to music. These were very difficult times because taking things from him didn't work and discipline would usually set him off. He was fighting for any kind of independence. Joshua's interpretation of independence was control and power.

In that instance, his storytelling and imaginative skills took a turn for the worse. Even though I wanted to think Joshua would never threaten another living being, let alone an animal he loved, I also knew this was a pivotal moment when we realized he could do harm— whether on purpose, in jest, or by accident. Hormones have the potential to turn the best of us into animals. When you're a testosterone-addled teenage boy, the unpredictable can happen. Add trauma, PTSD, and a master list of psychiatric disorders, learning disabilities, and medication, and these kinds of situations can turn from harmless to hazardous very fast.

Before the day Joshua threatened our pet dog, we had absolutely no doubt that this boy loved animals. As a child, he drew them in his notebooks. He obsessed over horses and even made up those colorful tales about owning a dolphin and a bull. But as a teen, he started to realize that animals can have real, visceral feelings like humans. Animals can predict moods. As Joshua got older, his mood swings became more and more difficult to read or to manage. But our rescued Jack Russell Terrier, Cassie, was a master at absorbing and reflecting his emotions.

It may sound crazy, but we took this dog to a veterinarian who specializes in mental health for canines, and Cassie ended up on Prozac. Maybe it was the stress of being a rescue, or from coming to a family with an unusual situation, but either way, Cassie picked up on the energy in the house. She fed off of Joshua's emotions and could naturally sense, see, and feel what mood he was in. It was almost like having a highly trained special needs dog (although she had no formal training in such) that could sense someone having a seizure or cardiac arrest. If Cassie became uncomfortable, irritable, and rowdy, I knew Joshua was also going to become uncomfortable, irritable, and rowdy. It didn't take him long to figure that out, either. Once he knew, boy, would he stir her up!

At first Joshua thought it was funny to see Cassie yipping, snarling, practically spinning in circles, or ready to launch into an attack. She would get so out of control we had to isolate her from our other dogs so she would not lunge at them. Of course, when this started to happen over and over, it raised red flags for me. There's considerable research to show that children who hurt animals or want to hurt animals have a tendency to hurt or want to hurt humans.

In his teen years, Joshua's moods and behaviors would swing so drastically that one minute he could love being around the dogs like they were his babies or a group of little siblings to nurture, and the next minute, his hormonal rage would come out, and he would literally tell me he wanted to kill Cassie. "I'm sick of her," he would say. That one day on the balcony, he actually held her at knife point.

While the two of them were upstairs on the balcony, Eric and I were downstairs. To this day, we have no idea what set him off, but he started chanting in that strange voice, "Mo-o-o-m, I have your dog. I'm going to kill her." On the corner of the balcony, I could see him shaking furiously as he held her. He had a knife. It took everything I had to keep Eric from running up there. I knew we would have to treat this situation calmly, with gentle words, like a professional negotiator would when trying to de-escalate a situation.

On one hand, I was fearful that if we stepped closer, he would hurt her, and on the other, if we didn't do anything, he would do it anyway. This "talking him down" went on for several hours. By the end, we felt as drained as if we'd talked someone off the ledge. This is only one example of how dramatic his mood swings could be.

As soon as whatever trigger, impulse, or chemical imbalance inside him was resolved, his mood would click off. He would change courses as if nothing happened at all. "What movie can we watch tonight?" Joshua would ask as if nothing had happened.

Black and white, his moods could be on either extreme of the spectrum. Did he remember those intense moments, or was he disassociating? We think it was a little of both. Sometimes I tried to probe him about why he'd do things—and specifically this time, why he would do that to Cassie. But I knew making a moral lesson was sometimes pointless, as he himself didn't quite understand all the events. Our therapist advised us not to push too much, in fear of things escalating. We also never knew what trigger would be next. If the situation resolved on its own, he went about his business "normally," and I would not probe for the reason.

This created a lot of friction and turmoil. Eric wanted to discipline him so we didn't encourage bad behavior, and I wanted to understand the psychological implications of potentially triggering another event. My husband found taking away something from Joshua to be that right amount of behavioral reinforcement "I'm going to take away the

Gameboy or the Nintendo or the Playstation," or "I'm going to take away your books," or whatever it might be. Normally, this is a good disciplinary step for teens, but Joshua was not your average teen. His inability to step back into that memory, into what triggered him, and the sinister role he had played, would often compound his negative emotions, putting us all back in the trenches.

Sometimes I said, "Just let it go. Let it go." This was not a move of apathy, but one where I understood we needed to give him emotional space and back up.

As with many things in our marriage, it created a silent battle between Eric and me, because once these scenarios with Joshua were over, I just needed it to be over. I did not want it to continue in any way. I didn't want Joshua to continue building emotional intensity. Eric wanted to take charge and discipline him as one would a normal teen. This caused constant mental and emotional anguish for me. Again and again, I found myself caught between trying to save this child and save my marriage.

When I look back, I have no idea how I lived from day to day through this war, other than the fact that I consumed myself with a high-stress job, grad school, and the things I wanted to do in my free time. Charging through life ensured I didn't have any additional time to think or to allow my mind to dwell on what was truly going on and spiral into darkness. Joshua or Eric. Two contestants, one of which I was always on the verge of losing.

Through both battles, I didn't see any win. I thought, *At some point, I'm going to have to make a choice.*

Taking care of a teen with intense special needs was one thing. Nurturing a marriage was another. But how difficult to tell yourself you must make a choice between them at some point, and then to live with that choice facing you every single day. *When is the day going to come that I will have to make the hardest decision of my life?*

Again, school consumed my life, along with working hours on end at the hospital. At the same time, I struggled with the idea of Joshua going further downhill or getting worse than he'd been at the treatment center. What if he went into another zombie-like state, a drug fugue, or anything else if we increased his medication? What I wanted was balance—to see Joshua balanced, stable in his plan of care.

Throughout all of this, I became more resentful that Eric was not as stressed over Joshua as I. Plus, he got to travel for work, and umpired for baseball every single weekend from February through June. Part of me felt bitter toward my husband who had mental freedom, less frustration, and the opportunity to remove himself from our home situation.

Now I look back and think, "That was his way of escaping and coping with this life, and what was going on."

It's hard for me to judge or blame him. It's the same thing as when he sought out other "people" that he might be able to help, and it just so happened that those other people were women. Eric felt at a loss for not being able to help Joshua and not being the dad he thought he should be. Outlets helped him deal with the pain of hopelessness and disciplinary stalemates.

Oftentimes, I was at home dealing with all of it, but in a different way. Of course, Joshua and I did have weekends that were calm. We relaxed together, and no animals were threatened! Joshua's imagination usually did revolve around animals, but in a good way. Since early childhood, he loved horses, marine animals like dolphins and whales, and domestic pets. The hours he spent tracing them on paper (sometimes he would trace a whole animal family of them) and learning about wildlife from books (primarily through the pictures) spoke the exact opposite of threatening an innocent pet. In his mind, animals represented everything he always wanted—freedom, freedom to be himself, and to run wild.

"I'm going to have a lot of animals. I'm going to save all these dogs," he would say, so sure of his future.

He would hate it if we passed a stray dog. At one point, Joshua would get so emotional, I would start carrying dog food and water in my car so if we saw a stray, he could set out a handful of food and a cup of water. We didn't always walk up to the dogs, but he would set it on the road or curb or parking lot, so he felt a little better having helped that animal. He connected with that because *he* felt like a stray, a rescue, a wild-yet-domesticated animal. He had known what it was like not to know where his next meal was going to come from. He hadn't known if he was going to be out on the streets. There was a connection between him and any stray dog.

We tried all kinds of things to socialize him, help him deal with his emotions and develop coping skills. One of those ways was through a riding school close to our neighborhood. I worked with them doing equine therapy, but that's not what we called it with Joshua. We called it "riding school."

They used a special horse that was therapy-trained for special needs kids, and he went there at least twice a week. We saw an improvement in his ability to cope and regulate emotions. It wasn't a complete success since instability and the chemicals in his brain would sometimes just take over and he would still have mood swings.

We had to stop taking him finally, because Joshua had a heated outburst at the riding school—a start to many mood swings. This was a phase he was going through, but he started calling the trainer, a young girl, all kinds of foul names.

I'm not sure he understood that kind of behavior was going to have a consequence that would impact him in a greater way than if he had been able to control himself. When he stopped working with horses, I was heartbroken because I felt this therapy truly helped him understand his own desire to be free while at the same time broken-in, trained, and understood.

Joshua still could not read, even as a thirteen-year-old. Even so, we had some lighthearted moments with him to remind us he was innocent and meant well. Some of the things he would say were part of his coping mechanism. For example, my grandmother would send him a Christmas card every year, and she would write his name on the envelope in cursive—very old school!

One day he told us, "I can't read this. Grandma always writes these cards in Christmas writing, and I can't read anything with Christmas writing."

This has become a light-hearted family joke, and to this day if we read something in cursive, we'll say "Oh, this is Christmas writing. Joshua couldn't read this!" The irony was he couldn't read anything. He couldn't read print either, but he used "Christmas writing" as his way of getting out of admitting he could not read.

We didn't mean to laugh at his expense, but Joshua never seemed to care—to him, it was the simple truth, *I can't read!* Other things, however, were a major source of sensitivity for him.

As a teen, Joshua didn't have the freedom other kids his age did—to go to sporting events, or hang out at the mall with friends, just he and the kids. He would hear these conversations at school, and that's when he became more and more difficult to live with—more belligerent. It was at this time that he threatened Cassie. Usually, the rebellious comments lasted only a couple of seconds, and then he would move on.

Part of that was hormonal mood swings, and the other part was discovering how different he was from his peers. Often, Eric and I would sit down to conversations centering around plans for Joshua's future and what his adulthood would look like. He overheard some of these, and though we never said anything bad like wanting to get rid of him, I think he began to really worry. And it made him wonder what his future would look like compared to other teens. During another heated moment, he came after me with a frying pan, but thank God Eric was home to stop him. Would he have hit me with it? No, I didn't want to believe it was possible. Was he unable to communicate and regulate his emotions? Yes, he was unable.

I always took the role of optimist during these events. I believed that the love and bond that we had would overcome anything. If Joshua got angry, it was going to be okay because I was his savior and emotional coach. Being the calmer one, the stronger one, I felt was my place as his mother.

Some of the most disappointing moments came when I realized that though I tried to support Joshua, it didn't mean I could keep him out of trouble. One example was when we got a call because he had completely destroyed a classroom one day. The police had been called in.

There are no words to describe what it was like to watch my child, who I knew couldn't fully understand or manage what was happening to him, be put in handcuffs in the back of a police car. There are no words to describe that helplessness. No one can completely understand unless they have lived it and know Joshua.

I continued to believe that he would not hurt anyone. I didn't want to allow myself to believe anything else because that was just way too damn hard. Eric, on the other hand, who was not necessarily pessimistic, was being very *realistic* when he felt that Joshua *could* hurt someone.

Sometimes, that felt believable. The older Joshua got, the bigger he grew, the angrier he became, and he now had the physical capacity to really hurt someone. The growth problems of before were out the window, and he was on his way to standing six feet tall.

It's hard to even talk about those times, knowing that the police would be called when Joshua got into trouble, and they would have to intervene. This was before publicity abounded on how the police handled people with mental health issues who were in a crisis—let alone a child in a crisis. They shouldn't be treated the same as adults.

We had to really watch Joshua when it came to food. Since he'd been denied food, among other things, as a child, he developed chronic overeating. We put a pool door alarm on his bedroom door because he would go overboard. I would buy packs of cheese singles, and he would sneak out, get them, and eat the entire pack. We'd find the wrappers in his pillowcase and under his mattress.

If we bought any kind of snack bags of Cheetos or Doritos, he would eat every single one. It was unhealthy and he developed severe stomach issues. This had begun when he was about nine years old. The pool alarm was not only to alert us about food pilfering, but also for his safety because he would tell us, "I'm going to leave to hunt the wolves in the middle of the night." The wolves took on another new meaning. Were they his insatiable hunger?

There were still physical issues but also emotional and mental issues with the release of anything from his rectum—all stemming from his early childhood trauma. He would become so constipated that his stool would be like the size of a baseball. I don't know how he passed it. At one point, Eric had to go buy a snake for the plumbing because every single time he went to the bathroom, it would clog the toilet. Eric was constantly fixing the toilet, and I was constantly controlling Joshua's diet.

Because we regulated his food, Joshua felt like we were punishing him by not giving him every single thing he wanted to eat. I would try to explain to him, "Joshua, you get three meals and several snacks every day, we've never said, "No, you can't have something to eat. But we can't let you hoard food and overeat like this."

It was a strange phase, one that inflicted mood swings on all of us. When you're going through something like raising a special needs child, you can't make sense of it, and you're just so frustrated and angry. There doesn't seem to be anything you're doing that's helping them. With Joshua, if he wasn't threatening someone, it was the food hoarding, or the peeing all over our room, just one thing after the other. Even when we were having a good day or moment, it was so hard to really feel good about it because we were always waiting for the other shoe to drop. It wasn't doing Joshua any good because he could tell we were always on guard. But we wanted so badly to enjoy that moment and think, "Maybe he's turned a corner."

Eric might say, "Rhonda said that every other day: 'It's gonna get better."

I really wanted to believe that. If Joshua began to feel things were getting out of control or he wasn't getting what he wanted, he would spiral out of control almost unconsciously. Some of these issues seemed as if they'd come right out of the handbook used by health professionals to diagnose mental disorders, telling what signs and symptoms someone might show: impulsive, repetitive, and obsessive behaviors, all linked to control.

Concerning discipline, I was not a strict parent. Eric was the disciplinarian, and I struggled with that dynamic because I wanted so badly for them to connect. Because of his special needs, Joshua did not take well to discipline, and he had no coping mechanism for it.

If something did not go his way, he would completely fall apart and would be unable to regulate—to identify his emotions, what triggered them, and manage them himself. I had a way of connecting and reasoning with Joshua that Eric didn't have. I'm not saying he did anything wrong, though. It was just a different dynamic, and part of that was related to what I had experienced as a child, and I could identify with what Joshua was going through. Despite the code red scenarios, the situations of danger and emotional escalation, of mood swings, screams, and slammed doors, I knew as his mother that this child only wanted one thing—to have control of his life, to have a voice.

❈❈❈

FIFTEEN

THE CONNECTION

"I am not what happened to me,
I am what I choose to become."

—*Carl Jung*

It's hard to imagine what being abused feels like until you've experienced it, whether verbally, emotionally, physically, or sexually. Until you get out of it, it's like a fog, a dream-like state. It festers and grows. It burrows down into your memories, undermining your self-esteem to your very core. It meddles with the way you live, think, and communicate with others.

One of my friends was in an abusive marriage, and it seemed hard for me to connect with her exact feelings because I had never lived through a situation of physical abuse in a partnership. Like many, I had that typical response of "just leave!" and based that on my first marriage where I did, indeed, leave emotional abuse. It's a whole different world when you're being told you're not good enough with a fist rather than mere words. In his early years, Joshua very likely knew many angles of abuse—if not all of them at once.

Eric found it hard to relate to what childhood abuse does to the developing brain, never having experienced any. After many years, I was able to unravel what had happened to me. Those days staring at the bathroom sink, the chipped white paint, the faucet dripping at my grandparents' house—it was a focal point in my memory for a reason.

It started with little things when I was between five and seven, and I confused it with affection. It was incredibly confusing as I didn't really know what it was like to have a father. Even so, it didn't feel "normal." I was desperate to have a father to love me, so I was willing to do almost anything for that love.

When my mom left us, and we were all split up, I found myself in my grandparents' house. I loved, no, *idolized* them. Since we'd lost our father, my grandfather was the closest thing I knew to a father.

While my grandmother worked shifts at the glass plant factory, he began abusing me. It started with small things like "Come sit next to me." Of course, I would. I would give him whatever attention he wanted. He was my grandpa! He saved me! He and Grandma rescued me.

I never told anyone until well into my adulthood. There are only a few people who know this. To this day, I am still scared that people will not believe me or will blame me. This affected my relationships and made me susceptible to other abusers. My mom's husband, Tim, abused me as well. It confused me about healthy sex. I eventually sought affection and acceptance through sex. Looking back, I might call myself a seducer as I desperately sought affection and acceptance. My self-esteem was caught up in my sexual nature. Touching meant attention.

Back then it became about *me* touching *him*, and my grandfather would take me into that small, cramped bathroom with white sink, where he would show me how to help him ejaculate into the sink. That's why I always hated going in there and looking at myself in the mirror, looking for the little lost girl behind the mirror. At the time, I remember my mind and emotions processing this as deeply wrong and equally sinister. *This doesn't feel right. I don't think I'm supposed to do this.*

But my mind was so conflicted: *These people saved me, and if it hadn't been for them, who knows where I'd be?* I knew survival, and what it felt like to be abandoned. If I said something, where would I go? The sexual abuse stayed in the realm of him touching me, rubbing against me, but he never penetrated or touched my private parts. That, I narrowly escaped. Though when my mother and her new husband Tim came back from their elopement in Tennessee, and we all reunited in an apartment my grandmother set up for us, a new kind of abuse got directed at me. He began to touch me.

"I know you think this feels good. You should tell me that." He always spoke sweet, too sweet to me, from the very beginning.

What my mom saw in Tim was a mystery to me. I think he was her escape from her abusive, controlling relationship with Pete. My mother needed a man, and she would admit to that. Although, he wasn't the best provider and was unemployed until my uncle got him a job at the local pressed metals plant. Tim was in the picture for the next 15 years until he left unannounced one day. Issues in their relationship came up because of her extra marital affair. I was glad Tim walked out the door, even if he had stopped abusing me years before.

Many nights, I would pretend to be asleep when he fondled and touched me. No penetration happened, but touch—so unnatural, sickening, leaving me feeling dirtier than before—brought on new waves of shame. *I must be the worst girl in the world to deserve this—again.*

Everyone would cheer me on, not knowing the full truth: "Oh, you're Grandma's favorite. You're the first granddaughter." That idea was so conflicting to me, and I thought, *If I'm the favorite, such a prized and precious girl, then why is this happening to me?"*

My grandfather only stopped after I moved out, and only to have it start immediately again—one predator to the next—with my mother's new husband who was supposed to honor her and protect us. I now had three men in my life, one gone, and two who abused me, to leave me in this world with these feelings of being abandoned or used. Finally, one night, during one of his too-close hugs, I told Tim, "I don't want you to touch me anymore, and if you do, I'll tell." Tim was scared, so he stopped. But I think he moved on to my younger sisters. I felt guilty when around him and my mom, as if I were a mistress of some kind. Imagine that, the victim feeling guilty. That three-fold dynamic confused me, and I never knew if my mom suspected, which felt even worse that she wasn't protecting me.

Though I don't have proof, I think it started up again with Teresa and Tanya after I stood up to him. Pedophiles usually target the ones they think they can manipulate to keep their secret. As an adult, I was riddled with guilt and thought, *Could I have done more to stop him from hurting them too? Would Tanya have turned out differently? Would we be in this terrible situation now?"*

I remember one time I noticed Tim pulling Tanya on his lap and I could see her wince. I could tell there was something off about their relationship, but I tried to ignore it because I was scared of what it would do to my mom. Would he kick her to the curb?

All of this gave me insight into the shame and lack of control over yourself and your situation. So I could relate to what Joshua was going through. Despite our issues, and what Eric and I disagreed about with discipline, behaviors, and solutions, I knew that abuse makes you a different person. I knew it was a heavy anchor to carry, and he needed someone to help him do that.

Many times I thought, *This is why God has put me here on this planet. This must be the great connection.*

In all of the events I might not have survived, like a car accident, abuse, abandonment, or anything else tragic, I was alive and on this planet to help Joshua. Although sometimes I wanted to cry, scream, and give in, I was driven to help him and figure out the great mystery, this answer to his own unique level of healing.

Raising Joshua from a young child to an adult was more difficult than the average parenting ups and downs. Though I'm not saying parenting in general isn't difficult, we had a child who had seen what millions of children have over the world—abuse—but in his own individual frame of mind. Joshua, aside from therapy, medication, treatment, needed empathy, and someone to "get it" even if he couldn't explain himself.

Many times I thought, *I'm his mom now, even though I didn't give birth to him. I'm a nurse—a pediatric nurse, and yet I can't help him.*

No words can describe that sense of failure. It was beyond measure, beyond speech—a realm of hopelessness, a tide that turns and comes back. I knew if I wasn't going to help him, Joshua would not survive the world. He would not grow into a young adult. He would never be even remotely independent or make it on his own.

Seeing him suffer wasn't anything I even wanted to contemplate. I felt that if I had survived so much in my own past, gotten this far, made something out of myself in this world, then I could be his foundation, his source for help, love, and wisdom. Joshua and I had always been connected through blood, but we were also connected to that one thing so many of us try to escape—pain and our past. Although I couldn't wash mine or his away, I could move us both forward.

***

SIXTEEN

DARKEST HOUR

"The darkest hour is just before the dawn."

—*Proverb*

About nine months or so after Joshua came to live with us, I began to have an increase in migraines. These had started for me around age fifteen but increased to multiple times a week. Over the years, I tried every medication on the market.

When my home life had dissolved, when Joshua's behavior had spiraled, and my marriage appeared to be going down the drain, a doctor ended my pain with a prescription for an opioid for breakthrough migraines. I've covered what happened from there, but I do remember that time as my darkest hour.

After I'd taken the opioid a couple of times, I realized there was another advantage to the drug: a sense of wellbeing. I also discovered that washing the pills down with a beer emphasized the euphoria. I felt like I could get through the evening, and whatever kind of chaotic, emotional whirlwind was thrown my way. I only took the pills after I got home from work, but I convinced myself I needed them to make it through the intense conflict.

Day after day this was the routine—a beer and a few pills. I was like many people who get caught up in prescription drug abuse.

For a couple months, this went on until a fateful day when the build-up of narcotics in my system while driving home from work put me in danger and potentially the lives of those around me. It was the same drive I had made for years—and as they say, "I could do this in my sleep." Well, that happened. I suddenly "came to" and was driving on the side of a golf course—a golf course I had never seen before. I realized I had gotten off at the wrong exit and had driven more than a mile off the road onto a large stretch of grass. This is when it hit me: stop this immediately, Rhonda, or you won't be around to raise Joshua.

Although I stopped the drugs, I still needed something to get me through while trying to cope with keeping the peace between us three, and the intensity of being Joshua's parent. That would be a shot of reality. One image from my memory made me hold onto hope: that little, scrawny boy in his underwear and superhero t-shirt waving goodbye to me. When would be the next time I'd wave goodbye to him again? I began to question if my Vicodin use was going to speed up that process and irrevocably change our lives.

I tried to convince myself it was ok to take the painkillers because I was not taking direct care of patients, but I was taking direct care of Joshua. It was, after all, prescribed to me. It didn't feel dirty or morally wrong like a street drug. I convinced myself I needed it for migraines and not for the deeper issues I was trying to numb. No way would I allow it to happen—to say goodbye forever, and that's what kept me going.

Sometimes we all have a "black out" moment before we truly see the light in our lives. This could translate to peak substance or alcohol abuse, a point of reckoning in our repetitive behavior or trauma, or anything that completely clouds our judgment of what's real or not. When we reach that place of no return, seeing how close we are to an end, it can be an unintended go-ahead to true healing. Suddenly, I was brimming with gratitude about being able to raise Joshua. Yes, we'd had the best and the worst times, but I had to reexamine everything from the scope of his perspective—he truly had the worst times before we came into the picture.

Joshua's life and our family's way of life was worth saving. His past trauma and present mental health issues were never his fault. He couldn't be held accountable. But I was accountable for helping him through it. I wanted to believe I could fix it all for him.

Constantly, I needed to keep my resentment in check. If I didn't, it got bottled up, pressure built, and finally exploded onto the person closest to me, the man at my side, Eric. I was torn between expecting more of Joshua or more of Eric: "Which one of you needs to work on your behavior more?" Though I hated myself for feeling this way, I was angry at them for not stepping up and trying too—I felt all the effort was on my part. So, I looked for ways to cope.

People on the spectrum cannot perceive, reflect, or understand emotions or social cues. It's not their fault. And you are not wrong for wondering if your loved one is a narcissist, or perhaps even has socio-pathic tendencies. You might be riddled with anger, frustration, or feel you're living in a constant loop of emotional replay. Please know that most of the time, you can teach a moral lesson and make a point, but don't expect them to acknowledge your pain. Save that expectation for a trusted therapist. As a caregiver, you are their *voice*.

The thought that always kept me from going under was *If I give up, who will be there to speak for him?*

Thinking of Joshua as a young teen, then an adult, a fully-grown man, I tried to picture his future without Eric or me. I would never allow someone I loved to be out on the street or to feel unloved or unimport-ant. Even when my mother and I trekked through some rocky times in our relationship—with all my resentment, anger, and betrayal at her abandonment, for her having left such wreckage and bringing in even more trauma with Tim's abuse—I knew she needed me in old age. It didn't matter why, when she needed me, I stood front and center for her. This illustrates how deep a child/parent relationship can go. A per-son may have a desire to help and to protect, regardless of past mistakes.

We often hear news stories where parents are reluctant to turn their children over to the authorities. Although this may clearly be the right decision, especially in cases of crime or homicide, it's usually a basic instinct to want to believe in the child's innocence, or to get exten-sive legal help to prove otherwise. I had wondered where I fit into that realm—would I try to protect Joshua, as I had in the police station after he'd threatened my sister Allison, without any kind of reproach or serious consequence for his behavior? The point is, a loved one with a cognitive disability cannot be held accountable by society, either. You can try to instill humanity, rules, or right from wrong. But you also, as their parent, hope you know what that child is or is not capable of on a deep level.

I knew Joshua was capable of great things on a small scale—reaching out to hug someone, to tell them they mattered, to use his voice for good—and that's another aspect of him that kept me going. Always think of the small scale when it comes to a loved one in this position and remember to tell them the little things about them you appreciate.

So much of nursing goes beyond medical treatment, medication, and a plan of action, to letting people know that you see them and their pain. Good nursing is a bedside service of nurturing the patient through the hardest times in their life. Talk to many nurses and they'll say their burnout moment wasn't the physical labor of the job but the emotional distress of being someone's rock, their voice, or their source of stability from the moment they walked in the room. Patients depend on you to guide or assure them. A doctor's job is to give results or a diagnosis, but a nurse's job is mostly to stick to a plan of care and do it with a caring heart. Sometimes, nurses grow cold or cynical with this task, treating patients as bodies, numbers, or as if they are almost dead. This usually means they're disassociating from the full-time job of being an emotional caregiver.

I began to see the correlation with my own situation. Between work as a nurse, school, and acting as referee and soldier at home, I wanted to "clock out" at times. Prescription drugs or drinking became a means to doing that.

Being able to see why you're zoning out is key. Whether you're a nurse or a parent, it helps to remember why you took this role in the first place. You can be the voice in the dark.

When you're in the darkest times, remember to find a healthy way to deal with the issues. For some people, that's a walk in the woods, or a stroll by the beach. Joshua loved the water. He especially loved being in the pool or the hot tub. Being in the pool was a calming experience for him, almost like meditation. For me, too, it became a source of restfulness and peace. Water is an ever-changing substance, so much like human emotions. That's why the two of us were drawn to it.

One clear, cool evening in Houston I made some hot chocolate, and Joshua and I sat in the spa. We soaked and relaxed and began to forget about everything else. It was then that I asked Joshua if he was happy. In the moment, in his happy place, he nodded. I told him I loved him. I told him I would do anything for him, and I would always be there for him. From that night on, I vowed to work hard at being the best mother to him. We looked up at the stars, the atmosphere one of wonder and harmony in such a chaotic world, and that became my light in the tunnel.

***

SEVENTEEN

JUDGMENT DAYS

"Good judgment comes from experience,
and a lot of that comes from bad judgment."

—*Will Rogers*

Finally getting the soccer ball. It's a crowning moment for any young child who wants a chance to shine in that sport. When that ball lands at your feet, you are front and center, all eyes on you. Just as eight-year-old Joshua loved being in the spotlight with his vivid storytelling, he always loved that moment during a scrimmage or practice: "I finally get to kick it!" But one time he didn't get that chance during a game, and the ball got tossed to another teammate. He didn't understand why. I had to step in and explain, and suddenly all eyes were on both of us—in the most negative way possible.

Once allowed to step in, I talked to the coach, who knew Joshua's situation. That's when the painful, sharp sting of mom-shaming began. Another woman on the sidelines barked loud enough for me to hear, "If only all of us had the opportunity to talk to our kids instead of having to listen to the coach." She used a scoffing voice. Then shot back more. "Why is he treated so differently?"

It took a lot for me not to lash out. Soccer moms and sports parents always looked on these situations as coddling, special treatment, or a reason to verbally confront me. Although restrained, my comment back was a simple statement: "Because he *is* different!"

Joshua's coach was well aware of the real truth and that underneath, Joshua had a hard time understanding rules, social cues, and being around male authority figures in general. Leadership, losing with dignity, teamwork—these are all positives in sports. Children with trauma, cognitive disorders and disabilities *do* need more support than other children if they participate in extracurricular activities, whether or not onlookers understand. From the outside, a child may not appear physically different than the others—as in Joshua's case. But underneath, he had a hard history, special needs, and a different way of seeing and coping with situations.

Many children with special needs either talk too much or talk too little. That's somewhat typical behavior for most young kids with no filter, or even shyness. But as these children mature there's a growing understanding of social cues or morals. There's a time to listen, to speak up, or to answer. Some special needs children may only use non-verbal communication like nodding, smiling, eye rolling, hand gestures, or stimming (repetitive motions or noises) that only parents or teachers might understand: "This hand clap means he's happy." Loud or busy environments usually over-stimulate any child, but it's far more likely for kids like Joshua. Their exaggeration, hyperactivity, or emotions come with no filter.

We might be at a grocery store and Joshua would blurt out something, catching the eyes of everyone in the produce aisle. But what he said would be completely out of context. As much as he loved to grab attention, sometimes it was unconscious or unwarranted. A lot of parents of special needs children fear these situations—being at the store, park, church, or anywhere that more decorum or social skills are required—because of what might be said or done. You must listen to what they say carefully and be ready to stop a situation that you know is about to happen, but others don't. You must be proactive to prevent a slow- moving though escalating scene. People on the outside might think you're coddling or have a spoiled brat on your hands, but they don't know you almost *have* to helicopter your child.

As his parent, I was the best person to step in and be that "go-between" voice—a coach within a coach. Many children need rules to be repeated often in order to learn what to do or not to do, but with special needs children, it can be exhausting how many times you must state a fact, a cue, or try to reason with them. As a child, Joshua was able to manage himself in such a way that people found it difficult to detect differences between him and the other children. As mentioned before, he once got livid with the trainer during equine therapy. Of course, I turned to witness a lot of eye-rolling and sighs from other parents— one of many times!

Even within the realm of special needs, many parents judge what should or should not be proper reactions from a child in public, at school, or in sports. Every situation is different, of course. As quick as people are to judge, I also step back and think, *I understand the turmoil, and how unique it is. How could they possibly know? I understand the difficulties mentally and emotionally. I want and expect the best possible outcome for my child and for who he's around. I'm supposed to protect him.*

When Joshua reached eight or nine years of age, the differences between he and his peers became evident. His cognitive abilities and learning disabilities showed up. He began to be judged by other parents, his teachers, and his coaches. There was a definite divide in how other kids and Joshua handled and managed themselves and situations. Other children could see past a disappointment like not getting the ball or needing to move on from a topic or subject, whereas Joshua could not let go.

It took me a lot of healing and maturing as a parent to get to a point where the looks and judgment didn't get the best of me. For the most part, out in public, Joshua looked like the perfect little gentleman— saying "please" and "thank you." He behaved better than the average adult! At times, he maintained what we considered good control over his mood swings, but I think he had anxiety and fear that acting up would mean abandonment—that making mistakes, or talking back, or doing what any normal child does would make us give him away as his parents had. Despite social confusion and burying emotion at times, Joshua felt he had to earn his place.

Joshua was desperate to be a part of a family, specifically our family. The difficulty with him was trying to determine whether he leaned toward sincerity or being manipulative.

Only a few months after he came to live with us, he asked if he could call us Mom and Dad. He also wanted to take care of the dogs and to be a productive part of the family. I think Joshua understood we were not going to give up on him, then.

When he told the school we abused him? "No, we won't give you up." When he set the garage on fire? "No, we won't get rid of you." After those seeming psychological tests on us, I think he began to feel secure of his place. The tough part for Eric and I was to let go of waiting for the other shoe to drop, or wondering if Joshua was manipulating us, and allow ourselves to enjoy the moments and appreciate them. I cannot begin to describe the emotional struggle. Even today I have this struggle with Joshua concerning truth—what he perceives to be the truth vs. the real and whole truth.

Many children from abusive backgrounds have a survivalist thought process embedded—to do their best or else risk losing things like their safety, a warm meal, or a roof over their heads. It's exactly how I felt being unable to tell anyone about my grandfather, or about Tim. *Will this ruin my chances of having a home?* Eric and I both knew emotions had been used against Joshua. And as his mother, I had to control my own feelings, especially when it came to anger towards others and their reactions. That, though indirectly, would be an example to him of emotional control.

An age-old, outdated adage says if you need therapy, it's your mother's fault. So I had that weight of guilt on me. Many mothers feel the gravity and guilt of their every action, their emotions, reactions, frustrations, what they say and how they say it, all playing into it. As a mother and a nurse, however, I had a dual self-reproach of "I'm supposed to fix him, and he's not supposed to be like this under my care," and "He's supposed to be a normal, healthy child with me." This all originated from a fear of being judged or misunderstood.

I wish I could say someone else out there understood our experience. At the time, I only knew our therapist understood that raising a child with cognitive and special needs, plus a background of trauma, can bring about emotions you never thought were inside you. Resentment, anger, doubt, and shame—we had all of those. We could be honest and open with the therapist, and she would be honest with us. She would tell us what the reality with Joshua would probably look like: what we feared, didn't want to think of, or what dangers could be present. She admitted it was not going to be easy and could destroy our marriage and any dreams of "fixing" him.

The "fixer" archetype had had a place in me long before. I was always the one to help, babysit, or corral Tanya to keep her out of trouble. Then in my first marriage, I was always the one to try and do it all—parent my stepchildren, work, and keep our lives together, until I chose another life. In my second (present) marriage it manifested in trying to fix our infertility issues, trying to fix Joshua's situation, trying to fix every little thing raising him, and trying to fix our marriage entirely. Many times, I felt like the emotional anchor, and my role had unconscious roots in trying to nurture everyone around me. My role as a nurse and caregiver began long before I ever cracked open a nursing textbook. It was second nature to me to step in and try to assist. Oftentimes I received a lot of judgment as a parent because of it.

For many years, I spent my time in therapy having these exact kinds of conversations. "How do I not judge others when I'm being judged?" I did not want to be judgmental of others, but I held onto a lot of anger about their criticism, despite how hard I tried from the innermost part of me. It's almost like being bullied as an adult. Because Joshua was unable to articulate, or was unable to count or read, it reflected on me: "What's wrong with *her*? Why isn't she doing everything she can to help her boy to be successful?"

Success, for us, meant going to an event, and Joshua didn't act out or throw down a huge chunk of emotion in public. This happens all over the world for parents with a special needs or developmentally-disabled child: a fear of leaving the house. You may be socializing them, but at the same time you're risking micro-traumas like bad days, temper tantrums, or judgment from others. Social situations are risk or reward. Mental health education still has a long way to go, though society is finally moving into a new era of empathy and understanding.

***

EIGHTEEN

REALITY HITS

"The best way out is always through."

—*Kenert Frost*

The day Joshua graduated from high school wasn't a typical celebration for a young man on the cusp of entering the collegiate world.

"I don't want to walk," he groaned, and neither Eric nor I pushed him toward a cap and gown. His graduation was a non-event. Joshua was twenty-three years old and had gone through high school through a modified program. Even after that program his reading and writing were at a bare minimum. Without these basic skills, the usual teenage rites of passage such as taking driver's ed, getting a driver's license, owning a car, or getting a job could never happen for Joshua.

During his high school days, that alone created an identity crisis for him. "Why are other kids going to driving school?" At least it helped that Joshua knew other kids whose situations were far worse than his, from his modified courses and after-school programs. We intentionally exposed Joshua to children who had experienced homelessness and severe physical disabilities so that he could begin to appreciate the small things in his life. We never tried to minimize what he had been through. But rather, we emphasized how having a loving environment could help heal him.

We would ask him to clean out his toy chest or his clothes closet and take him to homeless shelters to give these items to those in need. We wanted to show him the spirit of giving and help him experience gratitude.

Joshua lived with Eric and me until the summer of 2014, when he graduated at twenty-three. Like many young adults, even those who already trekked through four-year degrees, he didn't know what he wanted to do. Joshua wanted financial independence, autonomy, and adventure, but he knew he couldn't just decide to get a job and move out.

When special needs children become legal adults, and depending on the severity or type of disability, legal help can be crucial. You still must do certain things for them—sign papers, handle money and talk to medical practitioners on their behalf.

At one point, my brother-in-law drew up medical power of attorney, and Joshua signed those for us. We knew he wouldn't be able to manage certain things without our help: his medication, doctor's appointments, or check-ups.

Joshua would need help over time with many aspects of adulthood. How would he transport himself to a job? Would he be able to ride a bus and do it safely? What if he talked to strangers and was fooled by one? Would he work consistently and not let his emotions get the better of him during a tough customer situation?

The tantrums of his childhood, or yelling at a teacher, were heavy enough situations. What we all faced now that he was an adult was many times worse. As sweet and gullible as Joshua could be, he might take instructions from the wrong person, might have trouble with an authority figure like a boss or do something out of context that he didn't mean—like reach out and hug a female for affection.

There isn't preparation for every type of situation. You can try to teach them what to do and what not to, but these scenarios can go any number of different ways. A woman might understand Joshua's intentions by how he's speaking, his level of intelligence, and that he means no harm by hugging someone, whereas another woman might call the police.

Every day, we tried to teach Joshua something new about the responsibilities and expectations of manhood. The lessons encompassed all areas: social, financial, and emotional. This wasn't as simple as teaching him how to do laundry, save money, or keep up with chores. We told him over and over, "You can't do that" or "You can't say this" until our voices cracked. Sometimes, there was no getting him to grasp whatever concept we were trying to impart.

The relationship between the three of us reached a breaking point again. Anger skyrocketed, patience dropped, and some conversations between Joshua and Eric turned into heated arguments. I played referee between two grown men! Joshua wanted independence so badly. But we could not just send him out into the world and say, "Okay, good luck!"

One day in the summer following graduation, Joshua walked up to me nervously. "Mom," he said, voice fraying, "my chest is pulling me to Pennsylvania."

"His chest," I knew, meant his heart. The simplicity of such a statement made me half-smile. All these years, through so much trauma, Joshua experienced loneliness, a feeling that he was out of orbit, living in Houston. Our house would always be home to him, but even from his first days in school he felt like a simple country kid, ready to fish, or be in nature. His sense of identity was rooted in his birth state of Pennsylvania. Rural roots. Not like Houston.

Most of the people he felt he knew best lived in Pennsylvania. Even if he hadn't seen them in many years, nor spent much time with them, he felt a strong connection.

His grandmother and great-grandmother were still living and had their feet planted there. Tanya, too, still lingered around. I couldn't help but imagine Joshua's train of thought: "I have a whole other family. I have siblings. Family is family."

Even at a much younger age than Joshua, I remembered having that longing to be reunited with my siblings. I felt a little astray without them. Joshua had never gotten to experience siblinghood. Part of him would never forgive his mother. The other part wanted badly to be included, to be part of the family tree, and to have an ancestral home.

After a few weeks of thought, meetings with our therapist, and some sleepless nights, we began to map out the move. We called every single relative, even Tanya, who seemed nonchalant about it. Her son, after all, had technically been raised, and that part seemed over to her. Everyone seemed to be on board with this decision.

An emotional couple of weeks followed before the big day. Our relief, guilt, anger, and disappointment—all of it was wrapped up in love for Joshua and hopes for his future. Relief came with the thought of Eric and I finally having a little space and healing in our marriage. Guilt came from the idea of letting him go, though Joshua *wanted* to move and venture off. Anger came from hearing Tanya welcome him back after we'd done the huge, emotional bulk of raising him first. Disappointment, too, came from changing our ideas about Joshua's future —where we pictured him, or how we pictured him moving into this next phase of adulthood.

The three of us made the trek to Pennsylvania just in time for the Fourth of July. We'd packed what he would need right away and shipped the rest of his personal things. Just like that—a few big cardboard boxes, and Joshua was ready to settle elsewhere.

He held onto his grandiose plans of what he wanted to do once in Pennsylvania, mainly the fun of adventure and exploring. It had been over a decade since he visited his birth state, so he carried memories of Pennsylvania and the people he knew. We didn't have a clear idea of what trauma or frozen memories of early childhood might taint his return. All he talked about was the good times—country days, visits, and our vacations there.

Sometimes I wondered if Joshua had any idea that this was not a visit. That he was really moving there, most likely permanently. Some of his expectations might be broken.

The Fourth of July celebration in Brockway had always been a big deal. This year was no different, but for additional reasons. We stood on the lawn of my grandmother's apartment on Main Street watching the parade, chatting, and visiting with old friends. With an air of tension, Tanya sat a little off to the side, and no one spoke of the past. No one mentioned the years we had spent raising this boy into the best man we could.

I wanted that acknowledgment. *Do you see what Eric and I just did? That we raised this young man?* But I never wanted either a martyr mentality or to seem like a victim. And Tanya never gave us a thank you.

All I knew at the time is that when the parade stopped and the cheers died down, Joshua would be stepping into a car with her. What I felt I could trust about Tanya is that she would never let her son get hurt again, at least not physically. I wasn't so sure about emotionally or mentally. Would she understand her son the way we did? Did she know little things about him like the fact he called his heart "his chest?" As he buckled his seatbelt, I decided the two of them had their own world to catch up on—years of memories lost, facts about Joshua, his likes and dislikes. I wanted to believe that maybe my sister had an ounce of curiosity about her son now that he had grown into a man!

Our conversations leading up to this move had felt good, though I had an undercurrent of fear. All three of us felt more or less secure about this huge move after a lot of processing and doubt. Deep inside I felt the finality of it. *This is it. Joshua is no longer in our home. He'll always be under our wing, but not under our roof.* I felt a sense of guilt, nostalgia, attachment, and already I missed the boy I loved. He was becoming a man on his terms. Emotions flooded through me. For Eric, it was a sense of relief. This time, Joshua felt it too—a sense of relief, freedom, and a new horizon.

He did not shed a tear or cling when we drove away on a hot July day. Of course, like many young adults he had an idealistic view of what life would look like in this small, now not-so-familiar town that seemed only a hazy memory.

We had worked ahead of the move, along with his mom and Uncle Matthew, his dad Josh's brother, to get him a place to live. A friend even got him a job sweeping and stocking. From his excited phone calls, it appeared life was finally moving ahead for Joshua, though this would prove again to be a sort of honeymoon phase.

Reality would catch up. It would creep up, crash, and cave in. Joshua would finally find the voice to say, "Is this the world I was born into?"

Just like back home with us, he began to see himself from the outside—different, not like the people he called blood. Finding friends of like mind proves difficult in adulthood. You must find your place, and your tribe. For a special needs person who has always depended on others for finding their way, striking out into the world proves hard. For the first time Joshua realized how we had kept him protected and shielded from a harsh reality. It didn't matter where he chose to live, people are the same everywhere. They would still treat him as an outsider. They would not have the heart to listen.

❊❊❊

EMPTY NEST

"It is not what you do for your children,
but what you have taught them to do for themselves,
that will make them successful human beings."

—Ann Landers

A s if there were a ghost in the house—that's definitely how our empty nest felt. A week after Joshua moved out, Eric and I sat down to dinner at the table feeling the airy, cold silence, *Once three, now there are two.*

Unlike some parents who boast about how their child will move on, go to college, get married and start a family, or who simply hope they have the morals, ethics, and financial wit to survive, we sat on the edge of our seats. We had done the best we could. But we still worried, felt guilty, and dreaded a phone call that things had turned sour with Uncle Matthew, the brother of Joshua's biological father. Joshua had ended up in the same town as Matthew, and though they didn't know each other, Matthew had agreed to be of help.

Neither of us knew what to expect.

My anxious thoughts spun. *Is this real? Will it really be the two of us, and for how long? Did we do the right thing by sending him out?* That phrase came up at least once daily: "Did we do the right thing?"

Eric and I struggled with our identities—who we were both individually and as a couple. I was suddenly not the referee anymore, and Eric was no longer on defense. It took us at least half a year to figure out what to do next, but we made a conscious decision: we needed to take advantage of this time, the years lost, and really reinvest in the relationship. It might mean a date night, sitting down to talk, or having quiet, at-home dinners. We decided to make a habit of a weekly date night at one of our favorite restaurants and travel more together. We loved New York City. Even before Joshua had come to live with us, we had tried to go at least twice a year to the theater, shopping, and dining.

Life proved busy. Though we no longer had the elements of raising Joshua, I still had my stressful job while finishing my second master's degree, and Eric still worked and umpired. In between, we made every effort for each other. This became a time of reflection and vivid conversations. There were other impactful conversations, especially with some of my close friends who finally said these words: "It's not too late to try for a baby again!" Or "You could adopt!"

Those words haunted me. Eric's and my newfound freedom turned to retrospect and time lost. *Having a baby, having a baby* had been all I could think about during the beginning of our marriage, and now that I was older and had raised Joshua to stand on his own, the refrain changed to *I never had a baby. I never had a baby...* Regret that we hadn't done more—that we hadn't tried more (very expensive) fertility treatments returned. Though I tried to keep my mind busy with finishing my second master's degree, I became preoccupied with guilt. *Did we do the right thing after all?*

As those painful feelings began to resurface Eric wanted to do whatever it took to make me happy. But he wasn't one hundred percent sold on starting a family again. Even thinking about going through fertility tests and treatments brought on memories of stress, failure, and hopelessness from those years of trying—and would it be any different now? Would he have a chance at this age? Would fertility technology, and how vastly it has improved, work even better now? I still wanted to share this biological parenting experience with Eric, but we feared that our time for this had passed.

Back in the days when we first took Joshua in, we placed his needs first. As the years passed and our turmoil peaked, we knew it was not a safe environment to even try to bring a baby into. We already struggled to keep Joshua safe, sane, and well monitored, and the risk of bringing another child into that was not an option.

A lot of work had to be done in the therapist's chair as I asked myself, *How am I going to let go of the idea of becoming a mother, even if the chances are slim, without resenting Joshua?*

The concept of "just letting go" is not an easy one in general. I'm not sure the therapist ever had magic words, but she gave me the tools to let go and move on in whatever situation I found myself. What I really needed to sort out was the question, "Is this really what we want or am I only trying to fill a void?"

I remember a conversation Eric and I had over dinner one night. Eric had reminded me that we determined many years ago we would have a plan A and a plan B. Plan A was our careers and possibly a family of our own, and Plan B was the possibility of never having that and instead, raising Joshua. He said we'd been ready for plan B, and it was about time we began to appreciate what we have and be thankful for how much we had given Joshua over the years.

Looking back, we didn't want Joshua to think Eric and I not having children of our own was his fault. There were factors out of everyone's control. I had had an almost spiritual understanding that this, my nephew becoming my child, would happen. God did not intend Eric and I to go the traditional route of parenthood, and I had to see the greater purpose. If I'd had a biological child, it's unlikely I would have been able to take Joshua, and then where would he be? Would I have been a busy mom of one, possibly two children, and unable to even dream of taking on my nephew? How much more abuse would he have endured? Gratitude unfolded from these painful questions. Of course, all three of our lives had been intertwined for so long. Missing him was a daily ache!

During our empty nest days, Joshua and I would talk on the phone almost weekly in the beginning. I tried not to let him know how much I worried about him. He was striving to be independent, and I wanted to be supportive. He would always ask about Dad and his dog Cassie. "My girl," he would call her. He always had something memorable to say, things that stuck with me. On one call he said, "Mom, can you send me some recipes? I sure miss your Texas cooking."

Those are the moments I stopped wishing my life had gone differently or thinking in terms of an alternate universe. This one had provided plenty of life lessons, love, and gratitude. Along the lines of having my own children, I came to realize that I know it's easy to say, "Why won't you give this to me, God?" and even easier to say, "I'm being punished!" But going through these questions helped me release any resentment. I needed to say those thoughts out loud. I would reiterate to myself that Eric and I had known plan A was having careers, an established home, and trying for a child, and plan B, we were going to do what was best for Joshua. In the meantime, as we adjusted to him moving away, we had plenty of nieces and nephews to spoil.

Life as empty nesters settled into a routine. I was usually at work very early and home by late afternoon. Now striving to be successful, I had also recently received a promotion.

Just when I thought things in our lives had ironed out, with all working parts running smoothly, a kicker came in. I looked down to another text from a woman on Eric's phone. My stomach dropped as I thought, *This again.*

My memories flashed back to the pain of former days when I screamed inside, and the nights I numbed it all away with Vicodin. But this time was different. This seemed to be an innocent text that didn't threaten our relationship or make me feel the anger of betrayal again. I realized that weight was not mine to bear anymore. I let go of wanting control over Eric making friends. Our marriage had taken on a new mode of trust and security. Nothing could break us apart, even the hell we'd gone through in the previous years.

With that in place, the days felt smooth and fresh. They took on a positive sheen. I no longer stayed up late, thinking myself sick, or talking about Joshua as a means of deflecting guilt. Things were finally on the bright side. My dream job, financial stability, a secure, loving marriage, and even some time to work on myself through more therapy, self-care, and time with friends. Leveling into peace is what it felt like.

That, of course, would be the moment that family drama would step back up to the plate.

In Pennsylvania, the honeymoon phase with Joshua and his biological family ended. A few months after we had left him there, in late fall, I received a call from Uncle Matthew, explaining they were having issues with Joshua. He was angry all the time, sometimes violent or moody, and certainly not willing to take direction. It seemed he quickly began to alienate everyone. I am not sure what the breaking point was because I could only get a little information out of Joshua over the phone. The structure, routine, and emotional guidance he required was much more lacking than it had been with us. Lack of order is what sent him over the edge.

Kids and adult children with cognitive and special needs still need routine. They will always be children in that regard and cannot always form a schedule on their own. They need a structured environment, especially as they get older and want independence. Of course, it must match their cognitive abilities. You can try to help them establish the basics and give them the tools, but in the end, they must put them to use. Just like any adult child, they must figure things out. But this takes more processing, more time, and more patience with special needs adult children.

From so far away, we could only coach Joshua or our relatives through phone calls or text. Even if we were empty nesters, we were still on call, like any parents. We had been there before, and we would be there for the rest of our lives.

Though months could pass without a word from him, after seven years we grew more used to his absence. We felt gratitude for the days we got to hear his voice again, just to know he was okay. It made me think of what Joshua used to say when he would tell me everything, "Moms need to know."

This time, I would say, "I *want* to know! Please tell me everything."

❖❖❖

TWENTY

WHEN I GROW UP

"Adulthood is not an age,
but a stage of knowledge of self."

—*John Fowles*

"Mom, I need your help." The words on the other end of the line made my heart sink to my stomach.

Part of me wanted Joshua to figure it out and take a lesson in independence. Part of me was glad he'd asked me first and not a stranger.

Crying, stuttering, Joshua's voice broke. "I have nowhere to go."

In 2021, in the midst of the 2019 Covid pandemic, Joshua told me he was homeless.

"What are you talking about, Joshua?"

Joshua had been living with a friend and as I understand it, the friend never shared with his landlord that he had a roommate. Our son ended up kicked out and living on the streets.

To complicate the situation, Joshua had gotten into trouble with the law and was on probation. His probation officer told him he either had to get a place to live or would have to go to jail. I knew he would not survive jail. His only options were to be locked up, find a place to live, live on the streets, or move back home, uprooted once again.

Eric and I knew moving back with us wasn't a possibility. So, the only option that made sense was for Joshua to stay there and find a place as quickly as possible.

Within an hour, I'd called every apartment, every rental, every housing program that would allow me to lease an apartment under my name. But it had to be under Joshua's name as well. Based on his issues, he got additional assistance through the state, so we had to be smart about this. Maybe some parents would say to their child, "You gotta figure this out!" But we knew Joshua didn't have the cognitive ability to try, to problem solve, to find a solution in the real world. Even if he could start, there was no way he could finish something as drastic as this. Joshua was no longer the little boy in the superhero t-shirt on the side of the road, but part of him would always be just that—lost, searching, and helpless. No way would I allow him to be on the streets.

Throughout the years that Joshua had been gone, our calls would go in spurts. Sometimes we would talk once a week or once a month, but other times months would go by without a call. Not a day passed that I didn't think about him. Somewhere along the way someone taught him about Facebook, so through that platform I could at least stay connected. He also learned to use FB Messenger and I shook my head or smiled when I saw a message pop up "Hi Mom!" Since Joshua didn't read or write much, he sent voice messages or texts that were transcribed for him. He would usually use a friend's phone when he didn't have one of his own.

Once one of his friends reached out to me to tell me Joshua had left the apartment because he wanted a dog. I sighed deeply, wanting to scold him, "Joshua, you can't just leave a stable home only because you want a dog!" Pets were not allowed there, but Joshua wanted one badly. Most likely because he really wanted to care for someone and was starved for unconditional love. Animals offer that. Someone actually gave him a dog. This probably is what precipitated his leaving. A friend of Joshua's cared enough to call us.

"Joshua took the dog and is living in a tent in the woods," were the next words to send a shock through us. Between our phone calls and hearing about Joshua from outsiders, many inconsistencies arose as to where he was and what he was doing.

"Please have Joshua call me as soon as possible," I urged his friend.

Even though we lived across the country, there was always something with Joshua, and my stress was off the charts about his safety and whereabouts. Issues with an adult special needs child can be even more stressful than in their early days.

The message I want to get across in this book is clear: whoever reads this—whether it's a family member, loved one, or a friend—whoever has experienced issues due to a mental health illness, I want you to know it's okay to have different thought processes or reactions to situations like this. Even if you or your loved one is an adult, it's okay to react, to pull them back under your wing if they need help. Balance is key when raising a special needs individual from child to adult and beyond. It's a process that can be never-ending and exhausting. The process requires balance—understanding that person's complex medical and mental needs.

I had no anger or lecture to deliver to Joshua at that moment. My instinct was to get him housed and safe.

Situations like this, dealing with adult children with special needs, are like dealing with an adult child struggling with addiction. The parents may be in denial, and others might once again criticize the parents for jumping in to help or making excuses for their child. Only *you* know the unique situation, just as I knew Joshua inside and out. It becomes more complicated when you realize this person is only an adult in a physical sense. He tries to be an adult, but he only functions as a ten or eleven-year-old emotionally and mentally. I knew Joshua was still a boy.

It's hard for people who don't understand Joshua as an individual and just see him as a six-foot-three man. Joshua is the proverbial gentle giant. He may get angry and lash out, but in one sentence you could completely crush his soul. He is unable to explain to people what he feels, other than simple, curt statements: "I have special needs. I've been diagnosed." He can't understand his deeper issues or his trauma, let alone verbalize them.

When it comes to the business of living in the real world, people don't typically understand how to deal with a special needs individual.

The fact that they have been diagnosed has little meaning to them. For example, all the electric company needs is a customer to set up the account and pay the bill. That is their priority. They have no concept of "Oh, this person may need additional time to understand what you're asking them." Customer service systems do help the deaf and disabled but are not trained to answer or assist someone who might need additional help understanding the terms and conditions.

If you are his voice, the person who must go between your loved one and the real world, your place matters. Every child or adult, regardless of the level of their physical or mental capacity, deserves a chance. Don't let anger, resentment, or overwhelming emotional or physical stress defeat you. Your "expiration date" as a parent—the day your child becomes a legal adult or moves out—doesn't ever happen. It certainly does not mean they no longer need you. Your perspective matters. Your voice matters. One day, your story will matter too.

There are moments of relief. Over the last twenty years, people who knew Joshua will sometimes reach out to me and recall this or that story: "Hey, I was just laughing, thinking about that time…"

Once, my sister-in-law reached out to bring up a memory that brought hope and belief. "Remember when Joshua was trying to win a Gameboy at the arcade, and everybody said, 'You're not gonna win that!' and he won it! He said, 'I prayed to God and good Lord answered the prayer!'"

In that moment, we all remembered the serious, funny, innocent, and noteworthy of Joshua's character. He was praying to God to win a Gameboy—simple as that. Throughout even your darkest hours, you'll recall something light-hearted and remember a lesson learned.

Joshua taught me small life lessons I could not learn anywhere else. Nothing I could have learned if I'd had biological children—nothing in nursing or in my career would have taught me what he did. We underestimate the strength of these kinds of experiences our loved ones give us, as hard, painful, and never-ending as it seems.

Deep inside, I know Joshua's early days were similar to mine—full of abandonment, fear, and cruelty. I don't wish anyone to grow up having experienced any kind of sexual abuse, though I did. And it has become a part of my strength now. Do I wish it never happened? Yes, part of me does, but another part knows I would be a different person—with different sets of knowledge, instincts, and emotions. Would I have been able to connect with Joshua so strongly if I'd been on an alternate path?

We all struggle to find our voice. Even if your child, special needs or not, is going through the muck and darkness of reality, think as a child would think. Try to understand their fear, anger, and anxiety. Their difficulty trying to fit into this world.

One day, right before his time was running out with his probation officer, we found him an apartment. The landlord was very understanding about Joshua and his needs. We signed a year lease so he would not have to worry about where he was going to live. He wasn't thrilled about living far from places he felt he needed, like Walmart, but managed. Once again, we had given him the help he needed (whether he knew he needed it to begin with!).

The words "I need your help" can be positive in growing *and* growing up.

❉❉❉

TWENTY-ONE

FAMILY DYNAMICS

"Families are like branches on a tree—we grow in different directions, yet our roots are the same."

—*Unknown*

Joshua has two sisters—Anna, a year younger, and then a baby sister, Amee, five years younger. He never had much of a relationship with either of them. Amee is a half-sibling and came into the world when Joshua was under my care. Neither of us had much of a connection to her. With his other sibling, Anna, there was always the feeling that Tanya wanted to keep her but not Joshua. Unconscious resentment, anger, and jealousy built up in him. He was abused, abandoned, and pushed out into the world, while another child was born and cared for. To this day, he harbors some bitterness about it, and what sprang from it was a very rocky relationship between the two—one that caused fights and dramatic phone calls, and misunderstandings on social media.

For example, on Facebook the other day, Joshua commented that he wished Tanya well, and Anna came back with, "You shouldn't call her that. That's not her name. Her name is Mom." Anna has her own mental health issues, though she is higher functioning than Joshua, who was simply trying to be nice. Being nice to the woman who would always be his mother biologically but not in actuality, and being nice to a sister he never knew, was quite an emotionally mature step up for him. All these

117

years, it never quite clicked for him to connect with either Tanya or Anna, and I hadn't spoken to my own baby sister in years. I knew what sibling dissonance felt like, and that was only amplified with Joshua.

What had happened between Anna and Tanya—any kind of foster care situation, abuse, or involvement with Child Protective Services—I didn't know. From what I learned through my grandmother, I knew Anna had been part of what they call a "wrap-around program," which involved a lot of social work with her at home and at school. This little amount of support assured that Tanya never had to place Anna anywhere. My explanation of this to Joshua took a few times to sink in. Throughout the years, he would ask, "Why doesn't Tanya want me? Why does she want the girls, but she doesn't want me?"

My clarification was the truth. "It's not that she doesn't want you. She knows that what Eric and I can give you is better, and she wants better for you." He needed more help than Anna, more care, assistance, love, and understanding than what their mother could give.

No child wants to hear those words—why, how, or when their parents decided to give them up, but they still have a life-long curiosity about it, and self-doubt because of it. I knew that feeling myself, and how it lingers, festers, and eats away at hope. My mother walked away from us and left behind a trail of destruction for each of my siblings and me when we got split four different ways. Each of us felt a crippling sense of loneliness and isolation. I never wanted Joshua to feel that way. Even on the day Anna was brought home from the hospital, I took curious, one-year-old Joshua to see them and took him right back with me. He was already spending a lot of time with me then, and I never wanted him to even get a glimmer of being left out or cast aside.

After his other sister, Amee, was born, he met her on a visit to Pennsylvania. It was brief, and perhaps even a little dull for Joshua. He was less interested in his baby sister and more curious about Anna, since they were closer in age. It didn't matter if it was his sister, a friend, or an acquaintance, he was curious about people his *own* age—even if he didn't exactly think or do things on their level of ability.

As Joshua got older, it became more and more difficult to "act his age." He didn't have the same cognition or mentality of other kids his age. While they had moved on to new fascinations like more mature video games, Joshua was fixated on Pokemon or Mario Brothers, some things that according to other children had expired five or six years prior. Joshua hated that we wouldn't let him explore games with guns or murder, but because of his predisposition to violence or inability to regulate emotions, we didn't allow him.

Judgment from other kids for playing "baby games," not being able to read, or catch a certain joke—all of those hindered him fitting in, and that made it difficult for him to build relationships with kids his own age.

This was difficult for Eric and me because we knew this drew Joshua to younger kids. Even if they were a few years or a decade younger, he was drawn to those connections because of the child-like environment, and he could control the situation. A part of him wanted to make up for missing out of being the "big brother" type and being the oldest. But because of anything that could accidentally be said or done, especially as Joshua grew taller and bigger, his curiosity towards younger kids became a fear factor for us. Never did we let him play alone with a younger child—it was always under close supervision. Kids his age recognized those stark differences (his choice in games, humor, personality, cognitive ability) that littler ones did not.

When he was invited to an event and didn't fit in, we both felt judged—he by the other kids, and I by the other parents. Once, at a birthday party, a group played a game that required a lot of reading. Joshua, of course, had to give up and default. He didn't want to say out loud "I can't read" but it didn't take long for the others to find out. With the bickering, teasing, and lack of understanding that kids inflict, Joshua didn't get violent, but he did have a verbal outburst so heated we had to leave. Maybe he could not read but he could talk—and furiously so!

During those times, you are torn between helping your child get through a traumatic, real-life scenario they may remember for the rest of their life or avoiding situations like that entirely.

No parent quite knows how to teach a special needs child how to get through a social situation like this. You can try to help them, but you can't control the reactions of other kids who weren't taught empathy or understanding. It got to a point where Eric didn't want to even try to go to these kinds of situations that might cause anger, stress, or pain for Joshua.

Before even thinking about going to a neighborhood barbecue, we had to critique anything and everything: "Who's going to be there? How young are the other kids? How old are the other kids?"

We had to go through every worst-case scenario and what-if. That exhausting process made us give up and become isolated. Neither of us wanted to risk an outburst, accident, or Joshua getting his feelings hurt. Becoming more and more socially withdrawn wasn't good for any of us, but we had slim options. What Joshua loved doing was going out to dinner with older adults. He either loved younger, innocent children or older, mature adults who could see past any issue he might have. Our friends would go out with us and would be happy to pick restaurants friendly enough for our situation. This didn't help the fact that Joshua might not ever get along with other children or come close to understanding his younger siblings.

Family members are connected on a very unconscious level. Just as we search for or try to replace a missing or absentee parent, we often try to make up for lost relationships with siblings. We might try to replace them with a friend, a person their age, or try to submit to a younger or older role we fit into. In Joshua's case, he would be searching for that place as the older brother—the one who wanted to protect or help.

***

TWENTY-TWO

CONNECTION

*"The most important things in life are the
connections you make with others."*

—*Tim Ford*

Joshua loves sharing food pictures with people on Facebook. What's not to love about talking to people about good food? One day, he made a comment on a photo of mine: "There's my mom's good-tasting Texas cooking that I miss." To connect with me without using words, he leaves me songs and YouTube videos. These things represent how innocent and loving Joshua really is at heart.

Not long ago, I sat through a conference call about social media and RN influencers. So many positives come from social media in the medical and mental health realm: networking, providing resources and stopping misinformation. But obviously the opposite is true as well. Influencers may give mis-advice or share their opinions rather than medical facts.

Growing up in the 1970s in rural Pennsylvania, you can imagine the isolation we felt, but it was not about geographical location, or living away from a city, as much as it was not being exposed to what children are exposed to today. There are no time gaps in news stories. When

Joshua first came to be with us, there was less of a social media or technology impact. That did not come into play until later.

He grew up with the slow-coming onset of the digital age, which went from PCs and game systems to smart phones and apps. Sometimes that exposure can be positive and a platform for education. As a youngster, I had never been exposed to a culture outside my own. I had never even seen many people of a different race. Those things tend to keep one isolated as a young person, and you don't necessarily evolve as quickly as a kid living in an urban, multicultural melting pot. Diversity and information make you grow. Social media and internet access can help a child enjoy learning about other cultures and ethnicities, instead of living in a single dimension.

The opposite happens as well, despite all the information on mental health and special needs. Cyber bullying is at an all-time high. Suicide is the second leading cause of death for ages ten to twenty-four. More teenagers and young adults die from suicide than from cancer, heart disease, AIDS, birth defects, stroke, pneumonia, influenza, and chronic lung disease *combined* (The Jason Foundation, 2022). According to the American Academy of Child & Adolescent Psychiatry (2022), bullying, exposure to violence, abuse, and impulsivity, among others, are risk factors. Vaping, mixing drugs and alcohol, the dark web, and porn cause kids to develop and reflect destructive behaviors and sometimes to romanticize things like violence. With mass shootings on the rise, it's no surprise this generation has seen a social decline.

I do not envy parents raising kids today. Becoming a teen is hard enough without social media influence and mental health issues. If you talk to anyone in my generation, they can share coming-of-age hardships. But then talk to their children. Learning to navigate the world in the 2020s is not the same. Today, parents have the pressure of constant monitoring, which thankfully is made easier with parental settings, enforced time limits, and the use of firewalls. Whether it's social media, TikTok, video games, or dangerous challenges, these all impact how a child develops. More so with children of special needs. They won't always understand the blurry lines of the metaverse vs. reality and might mistake a simple joke or video for a known fact.

We kept a tight rein on what Joshua saw or heard. Although he didn't have anything like a flip phone or smartphone, his friends did. He had small moments of exposure that way, and it wasn't positive. Like many teen boys, Joshua was magnetically curious about pornography, and we worried that exposure might trigger feelings of his past abuse, or that it would misrepresent how relationships are supposed to be. His porn use came to the tipping point when we caught him using my personal computer in the middle of the night and it got a virus. I was in school at the time, and lost all my work, assignments, and research in one, clean sweep.

This, of course, led me to give him a huge lecture on cyber security. "You can't just watch anything because it can be garbage. Phishing scams, identity theft, and cybercrimes are real." All teens need that lecture, and especially those with special needs who may not understand the internet is almost like a place—not exactly reality, but with billions of people on the other side, eager to take your information.

These days he's well-versed enough to have a Facebook page. Someone also taught him TikTok, though with some things he posts, I have to jump in and say, "Joshua! You can't post something like that." He doesn't always understand the consequences and might post something like, "If so-and-so comes knocking on my door again, I'm gonna shoot him!" Joshua doesn't even own a gun. He simply doesn't grasp the power of words.

Connecting something he does or says with the result of what he does or says is a difficult concept for him to grasp. Morals, manners, and apologies—these are things Joshua might understand afterward and not before. "Maybe I shouldn't have said it that way." This holds true for many young kids and even young adults whose brains are developing. With the onset of hormones and mood swings, kids are quick to jump the gun—to do or say things without understanding the consequence. Again, I don't envy parents raising kids in a generation that is exposed to so much peer pressure with social media. For Joshua, it was difficult for him to understand why we protected him from more mature concepts. "Everybody is doing it, why can't I?"

Now, with Joshua a thirty-year-old, I constantly monitor his accounts and messages and say, "Please take that post down." or "You need to rephrase that." or "Don't post photos of you smoking and drinking! That's not a good look for you!" People know him as someone who takes medication, and the immediate question rises, "Why would he even be drinking a beer?" This all poses a challenge and a whole can of worms trying to protect him from what others can do or say in response.

More information about mental health and law enforcement de-escalation is also rising on social media. How to tell if someone is in distress, having a mental collapse or psychosis, or cannot verbally communicate a problem—all of this is gaining more traction. Still, you never know, and I struggle with guilt that I'm not there to speak for Joshua. I can't be his twenty-four/seven voice like before. I can't monitor birthday parties, get-togethers, or his work life. One thing he says could be misconstrued and suddenly turn into a violent threat.

An impulsive nature—that was one trait his psychologist pinned down immediately. Joshua cannot separate impulse from what will result. If a police officer stops him and he puts his hands in his pockets nervously, he won't notice the officer suddenly going into defense mode until a gun is pulled, and then he really knows! What the officer does not see is a thirty-year-old man with a huge build and height, but with the mind of a ten-or-eleven-year-old.

It's difficult to convince people of that until you spend time with Joshua and hear where his mind goes. He might blurt out something strange, seemingly rude, offensive, or otherwise socially unacceptable. In today's cancel culture, when someone miscommunicates or offends someone, it's even more important to look at the voice behind it and forgive. This creates a chance for empathy and communication, a real connection where grace is given. When I see Joshua has written a post using the words "gun" and "shoot," I *know* he won't shoot someone. He can't cope with or articulate anger. The average person, when upset, might go for a run or confront the other person maturely, but Joshua will say something point blank—no filter!

People on the spectrum with special needs of all kinds struggle with articulating anger. Joshua struggles with how to express anger, how to deal with emotions, reactions, and big changes. He might do so all his life. What I can count on is that he will try, at least try, and grow—because he wants to connect. Some people with special needs or cognitive disabilities become distant or avoidant. They might become shut-ins, recluses, or be quieter than most people for fear of burdening anyone. Although Joshua gets moody, he speaks up. He expresses his emotions, even wears them on his sleeve, rather than bottling them up.

When Joshua first moved into his apartment, he sent me a message: "Cockroaches have touched me, they have diseases, and maybe even COVID, now this means war."

He has a funny way with words, and you can't help but laugh. He also texted me about a mailbox for his apartment, and I told him he would need to get a PO Box. Very seriously, he asked me if he could just cut a hole in the door so the mailman can use that for mail. He was "desperate" because he was waiting for a package.

He would also send me sweet messages: "I love you too, Mom, and in my heart and in my soul, you are my mother that gave birth to me." And "I got myself a job, I'm so happy!" Despite our battles and struggles, I knew the most important thing in the world was for Joshua to feel connected however far away I lived from him.

Coming home after a long workday, it became my ritual to crack open my laptop and scan for messages or posts from Joshua on Facebook. *What has he said this time? What do I need to tell him to take down?* Sometimes this stirred up worry, but I always swelled with gratitude with the fact, *at least he talks. At least he doesn't stay quiet. This is an outlet for him.* I looked forward to his name popping up in Messenger and what insight Joshua had to share next.

✳✳✳

TWENTY-THREE

LISTENING

"When people talk, listen completely.
Most people never listen."

—*Ernest Hemmingway*

Going back again to that day at the police station, I remember the way the fluorescent lights beamed down into my eyes, hot with tears. I wiped my face and pictured my son curled up in a cold, damp cell—exactly where most of society might have wanted him. I stood at the front desk, choked up. I could barely get out a word. If a few of the right people had just listened and tried to understand him, none of us would be here.

Police aren't the only ones who should listen to those with special needs—though it's especially important for them, because they're carrying loaded weapons—but for anyone in authority who might perceive Joshua as a threat, or perhaps might become violent because they think he will become violent first. Think of a store owner, or a manager, who might hear him grunt out an angry word or two while skimming the shelves and call the police out of fear.

Most parents in Eric's and my situation are in a constant state of worry about social perceptions. Worry that something might happen to their child. When a special needs child becomes an adult, those fears are amplified. You can't always speak for them.

What our society can do better to listen to this next generation, special needs or not, is to use our eyes first. Pay attention to visual cues: someone stimming (use of tics and repetitive movements), their body language appearing distressed, or their movements looking either slower or faster than usual. Try to observe first and respond next. Joshua's demeanor would suddenly turn to anger, seemingly out of nowhere, as if a switch was flipped. But there would be signs I could recognize in him before his behavior changed: blank stares, disassociation with reality, confusion with his surroundings, or cussing every other word.

Some people find either observing or listening hard initially because our first instinct might be self-preservation or possibly to judge. Although Eric loves Joshua and always will, it's difficult for him to understand or relate. A person with varying special needs functions on different levels than the average person. They process, regulate, and express themselves in ways that most people don't.

For many years, something that bothered me is that when people see a child with Down Syndrome, they can visually connect how the child looks to a condition, and they don't jump to conclusions, judge, or make a predetermination of that person. But people like Joshua do not have a visual indicator. Since he is a thirty-year-old with normal features, judgment begins quickly, even from the first word or two out of his mouth. They might make a judgment on what kind of person he is, or where he is from, what kind of parents he has, and maybe even write him off as dense or troubled.

It's about trying to understand the function of their brains despite what they look like. The metaphor "don't judge a book by its cover" rings true. It's not about judging them in a positive or negative light; it's judging because he doesn't act or talk the way you would *expect* him to, based on looks. If you spend more than two or three minutes listening to Joshua talk, you begin to understand that maybe his neurons and synapses aren't working quite like yours. It takes a little more time and effort to understand that he's a troubled and immature soul. You don't have to get why that is, or how he became that way. It is what it is, and you need to take that into consideration.

When young adults like Joshua encounter authority figures who they likely have had an issue with all their lives, it's even more difficult because their first line of defense is to be resistant. Just like unruly children, they might say or do something they don't necessarily mean, but without understanding the consequences. People his own age in his adult life understand this. They know poking the bear brings danger.

Joshua has a roommate that is younger—in his early twenties—who is disabled physically and mentally. But because one can physically see it, he is treated differently.

Joshua is very drawn to people with disabilities because he wants to be helpful. Just like when he was an eight-year-old and saw a dog that didn't have any water or food, he wanted to save it. Compassion and empathy never left Joshua. It's the same when he sees vulnerable humans. He feels like he needs to step in and help.

Specifically, if Joshua sees they are more vulnerable than he is, he feels a sense of control and superiority, as if he's the man of the house. In this living situation with his roommate, he really is that. It's almost part of his fantasies coming true, to communicate his own purpose. To have a voice.

An ironic aside about voice: the very medications that are meant to help special needs people to experience better communication often literally impair their vocal mechanism!

By no means should we excuse people who need medications—they certainly do—but there's a sentiment of "Let's just give them Lithium or Haldo and be done with it." When you know someone has a very complex history of psychiatric disorders, as Joshua does, there is no one pill that solves the problem. Finding the combination is incredibly important regardless of age.

I think of Joshua, drooling and deafeningly silent, sitting in the chair at the treatment center. No one paid attention to the clear visual. This boy no longer had any voice, choice, or identity. For him to have any kind of stability, one that would create an opportunity for him to grow and learn, it was about finding the right combination of medicines.

We went through almost ten years of trial and error to find the best medications for Joshua, and a psychiatrist who understood pharmacology enough to figure out the right balance for him. We had a gallon bucket of prescription pills that hadn't worked. An entire bucket!

Some medications caused uncontrollable tremors in his extremities, and if you're a nine-year-old boy going to school, or trying to do basic tasks, that's not going to work out for you. Some made him too drowsy to function, or he'd get severe constipation, or be unable to eat, or suffer memory loss, or develop elevated liver enzymes. The number of problems and side effects were daunting. It became a constant struggle to figure out what was going to work and would have no long-term ill effects.

Even now, I worry all the time, "Well, how is his heart? His liver? His kidneys?" after years and years of so much medication. It had to be near abuse of his organs. Not intentional abuse, of course. His body has just been flooded with these medications in trying to find the right regime. I think it's important to understand that it's probably going to happen when you have multiple psychiatric disorders. It's even more important to find someone who can manage all those medications into a "cocktail" that's going to be the best it can be for him physically and mentally and yet not interrupt his ability to function.

Those days of experimentation were hell on earth. Every minute watching his little body and mind go through the effects of these medications that were *supposed* to help him. Any parent knows this as torture. Professional thought on Adderall and Ritalin are still very controversial. In my generation, I didn't know anyone at school on those types of medication. I'm not saying there were no kids in kindergarten and first grade that were on it, but there was very little known about ADD or ADHD. "Kids are kids," as they said, and there was a greater tolerance for what we would consider hyperactivity.

When Joshua lived with Tanya and was being bounced from school to school, they started him on Ritalin, and then changed him to Adderall. Here was a five-year-old addicted to prescription drugs! Again, I am by no means downplaying the importance of using it when needed for brain function. It's just a slippery slope of whether the treatment is really needed or is a cop-out—and what the child really needs is a good dose of talk therapy.

Today we see teachers under a lot of pressure to have large classrooms yet still ensure each individual child meets their annual exams and scores. And there's pressure on single parents economically, especially if they're living on one income and trying to manage all the co-pays that come with psychiatric treatment. Do those teachers or single parents have extra time to observe and listen to a child's deeper problems? There's no way I am going to judge. I hope, soon, someone will find a way for children like Joshua to get the care they need without having to jump through so many hoops.

The term "trauma-informed care" is new over the last decade, and it's gaining traction concerning how life events can influence psychiatric disorders, whether a person already has disorders prior to the trauma. I would say trauma-informed care and testing for adverse childhood experiences (ACEs) help families, teachers, and others recognize and respond to the signs and symptoms of trauma.

Once I heard a group of teachers mention that sixty percent of their students are on medication. I thought, *I did not even know six kids that were on medication growing up! At least that I knew of.* What has changed or happened in society that we believe there's a "magic pill?"

With computer or TV screens and internet accessibility, children's focus is already impaired. We should consider their environment before deciding to medicate them and investigate possibilities of past trauma. But we should also consider that their mental health problems might be linked to information overload and screens alone! We must ask ourselves, "Is this an *internal*—a brain function issue, or is it an *external*—or environmental issue either at home or at school?" *First* check whether there are factors in the home environment or routine.

In my three decades of nursing, with most of it in pediatrics, I've heard parents say, "Well, now they're not concentrating. Now they're not sleeping. Can we give them something for both?"

Sure, real sleep disorders can present themselves, but how about looking at a TV screen up until the moment they sleep? That literally sets their brains on fire, and it's impossible for them to shut down! Again, ask: is it an internal or an external issue? Listen for and write down various factors. Misdiagnoses and miscommunication in psychiatric disorders is at a record high. Miscommunication is a primary cause of anyone jumping to conclusions.

That long-ago day at the police station, fumbling for the right words to say to get Joshua out of lock-up, I ran through every possible way to make it clear: "He's special needs."

What got us there in the first place was a monumental error of *not* listening between two family members: Joshua and his Aunt Allison, my *fourth* sibling. Yes, all those years ago when I was thirteen, my mother had had another baby, and I never imagined where she came from and how I would once again feel betrayed by my mother.

No one in the world except for three or four others knew this big, dark secret—until now: Allison was the daughter of my ex-husband Richard.

When I was a fresh young teen, he was a charming seventeen-year-old neighbor who appeared to have a crush on me—but was secretly seeing my mother.

Imagine the confusion of having practically raised a baby sister and then unknowingly married and divorced her father! It doesn't get any more warped than that!

Even after taking up with my mom, he seemed to think he could have a relationship with me too, though at seventeen he was too old for me. Besides, I had no interest in boys at that age.

Two to three times a week, he would come to our house to visit me, or so I assumed. He tried to catch those glimpses of his secret love child, Allison, but didn't have any interest in admitting he was her father or participate in raising her. As young as I was, I had no idea he'd had a liaison with my mother. I only knew we had a new baby in the house, a new mouth to feed.

At Allison's birth, she had a round face with chubby cheeks, big eyes, and the sweetest button nose. She looked like a doll, and throughout her infancy, protecting her became my role. She was my real-life doll! While Teresa, Tanya, and I all shared a room, I wanted little Allison to sleep next to me in her bassinet. I felt the same anxiety, the same urgency to care for her as I had for Tanya. *Who will help her?*

Subconsciously, I was aware of the rumors about how much time the neighbor had spent at our house when Tim, my mother's husband, worked the three-to-eleven pm shift. As far as I know, Tim was unaware of the inappropriate relationship and treated Allison as his own. My mother was determined to raise Allison as his. I remember playing cards at my aunt's house (she lived next door) and hearing sly comments made about seeing the neighbor at our house until right before Tim got home. I could tell by the tone of the conversation there was something else going on.

During this time, I thought baby Allison was mine. One day I came home from school and noticed my mom had cut my three-year-old baby sister's hair. Crying and crying, I lamented, "Why would you cut *my* baby's hair? Why did you cut her curls off?" She was my baby, mine to care for. Many years later, Allison as a young woman would be mine to care for again.

I don't remember the exact year but at some point, my mom and Tim split up, and he moved back to his family in Tennessee. My mom and Allison lived like nomads, moving to a new apartment or a new house every six months or so. I don't know what would have happened if my grandmother hadn't been there to help them. This created a strain in my mom's relationship with her sisters, since they felt she was taking advantage of my grandmother.

Wherever they were, Allison was never without my phone number. She would save all her quarters and find a payphone to call so I'd know she was all right. I am amazed at the wonderful young woman she grew up to be, given all she went through.

While Joshua still lived with us, Allison decided to move to Houston to finish cosmetology school. Immediately, Eric and I said, "We'll help you," and we did, getting her through her last nine months of training.

Allison moved in with us. Of course, the family dynamic shifted, and the tension between Joshua and Allison was thick enough to cut. In his eyes, she represented a threat to our little trio. He saw how close Allison and I were with our long, complicated history. He seemed to feel *She's giving up on me and taking on a new favorite.*

It was at this time that I found out who her real father was, and Joshua heard and saw this played out like a bad reality show. "Who her father was" and "who he was to me" confused him. One day, he walked up to me and in a wistful sort of voice said, "Are you going to kick Allison out now?"

"No, Joshua," I answered clearly. "We are not."

As a young girl finding her way in the world, Allison knew how hard it was to leave our mom. At the same time, she knew her future only had limitations there. She held onto dreams of seeing the world and experiencing life outside of small-town Pennsylvania. She wanted more out of her life, like her big sister had wanted.

Not only had the dynamic shifted in our family, but sparks flew. Of course, I would not kick my baby sister out. Joshua's resentment grew.

Jealous, suspicious, going easily from one to one thousand in his anger, Joshua's moods created a lot more friction for me as the peacekeeper. Now that there was a family member in the house close to him in age, he felt a need to fight for his place in the family.

Sometimes Joshua saw Allison as a friend, an ally. But I became protective of her, especially knowing that my baby sister was the secret love child of my ex-husband. So many lies swirled around my head. My protectiveness made Joshua all the more resentful of her.

Most of all, I wanted my mother to tell her the truth. She was owed that. It was through a letter from my mom that I had learned the truth. I remember sitting in the red chair in our little study reading the letter over and over. Part of me was in denial. I hated my mom, I hated my ex, equally. I felt betrayed by them, and the fact it took twenty years for the truth to come out proved even more devastating. I demanded my mom tell Allison. She had a right to know.

It created torrents of emotion for all of us. Joshua felt Allison got more attention than he did and needed daily reassurance that I loved them both the same.

The arguments between them were typical sibling stuff: who was going to watch their show on TV, who ate the last slice of pizza, why he annoyed her, etc. Joshua was like a pesky little brother to Allison, and she often resented having to watch him. I was left to deal with an increasingly tumultuous relationship between them while also experiencing relationship problems between Eric and me. Our lives seemed like one big train wreck of personalities clashing.

Eric and I were at the breaking point when we found ourselves on a flight to New York City, sitting across from each other, eyes locked. I had to attend a work event and saw this as a chance for us to get away, while Joshua and Allison stayed at home with house rules and procedures in place.

I tried to picture a happy little scene where the two of them stayed away from each other—in complete silence, on separate ends of the sofa!

By this time in 2011, Allison had quit cosmetology school and we were helping put her through nursing school instead. She'd found her first job, and finally moved into a place of her own. I'd asked Allison to come back for the weekend, thinking they had outgrown any drama, as Joshua was twenty years old.

What happened that weekend would play again and again in my mind, and I would only hear what the policeman said:

"He had a knife. The two were in an altercation in the backyard and he threatened to kill her with it. Dispatchers were informed and we followed through with an arrest after tasing him."

While we were still in New York, three sides of "he said" and "she said" and "they said" (the police) came at me like daggers. I didn't know exactly what happened until later. All I knew was that the police came, and the pivotal point was that no one listened, Joshua included.

"She's not my mom. She can't tell me what to do," he had said, reverting to what most teens say, and in this case, he was one mentally—something Allison didn't quite grasp either. She told the police he wouldn't loosen his grip on a knife he pulled from the knife block in the kitchen.

As serious as this could have become, I knew the two of them and how far the drama could be stretched. Part of me felt Allison became theatrical, though I'm not saying the threat wasn't real. Again, he's a big guy, I get it! Tasing him, though, when he could have been easily talked down—that never had to happen.

Looking back, I'm grateful he took *that* blow rather than someone pulling out a gun. As I stood from the dinner table, my first thought rose up: *He's alone. He's isolated. No one is going to listen. He's not going to have his medication. What will this do to him mentally?*

Immediately, we dropped everything and got on a flight back.

Another aspect of having a special needs child who is also a legal adult, is that they often treat and charge them like adults, with no context. You can almost hear them thinking, *He doesn't need you here. He made that decision.*

Standing there in the police station, leaning on the table for over an hour amid my tears—begging and pleading—I had one hand on my phone (calling his therapist) and the other digging through my purse (for proof of his medications). "He's in there without these, and you don't understand what this is going to do to him."

They would let me talk their ears off, but it was a hard "No" on seeing or talking to Joshua. I had no choice but to go home at this point. I got a call later that he was sent to the county jail from the little city police department. They'd loaded him up in the middle of the night like a criminal. I'm not saying what he did wasn't wrong, but this was a multi-faceted error in judgment.

Angry at myself for trusting Joshua and Allison to stay alone together, angry at Allison for not just calling me first, I know to this day that that one event created even more trauma for him about strangers hurting him, for reasons his cognition couldn't figure out.

I have to say, though, it did a little good by teaching him how easily things could escalate if he didn't effectively communicate his emotions. Not only did he need to communicate better, but it upset me horribly that people didn't take the time to listen and try to understand. I thought *I* was going to be arrested for trying to make other people listen—causing a ruckus in that office, crying, and begging! I wanted to get through to them, "He doesn't have the mind of an adult. He's not who you think he is."

It sounded so easy: Allison was going to come live with us, and we were going to help her. What ensued was way beyond what we'd expected, and it cemented the fact we were glad we hadn't had kids of our own. That would have been a constant trauma for Joshua. What scared the hell out of me: *This could be our lives from now on. This is our reality with him. How many times will I be standing in front of a police officer? How many times will I have to explain what happened to him, and how he is the way he is? How many times do I have to save him? How many times?*

I had nightmares of that day for months. Joshua was remorseful, apologetic, and traumatized. He didn't speak the entire forty-five-minute drive home.

After that, Eric and I lived in a state of fear for years. When Joshua had first arrived, my husband thought he was going to be a bad parent, mainly because he felt as though he was unable to influence Joshua. We could not change this child but only help him. Sometimes those problems got worse when another person—like Allison—was added to the equation. Another fear was that we would never, ever be able to teach or even truly reach Joshua about being an adult. This only compounded when he got older. So many memories existed in our house—holidays, seasons, the good, the bad, and now that this sense of a police presence had pervaded our home, the extremely ugly.

I realized, as most parents do, "We did everything we could." It wasn't giving up, but simply realizing that we had listened. We'd been there.

We gave him and will always give him our love. It's the world, the others within it, who need to learn how to help Joshua speak for himself too.

It's not only police figures (though they certainly are primary because they're carrying loaded weapons), but anyone with authority who might perceive Joshua as a threat. Or those who might react with violence because they *think* he's going to be violent. I'm in a constant state of worry and a sense of threat that something may happen to him.

How can we all do better to listen to this next generation and people like Joshua? It's about listening and watching. Sometimes there are indicators in youngsters and grown people like Joshua which point to something else that may be happening in them, around them, or to something they're about to do. I think it's more than listening and observing, it's trying to understand. I know for some people that's difficult, and Eric is one of them. It's difficult for him to understand because he can't relate, but still, we must try to understand that their brains function differently than ours.

Sometimes the problems got worse when other people visited. When my grandmother, Joshua's great grandmother, came to visit, it was a free-for-all—and his behavior spiraled out of control. Though we had some pretty good or funny memories, there were moody, unpredictable turnarounds where we were scared for him and somebody else, and sometimes for ourselves. We couldn't ask anyone because no one had been through this exact situation before.

When his mother showed up and decided to take him back, it was difficult for us because we knew the result would be toxic; and sure enough, that came to fruition. He ended up in a treatment facility. Uncared for, unseen, unheard.

We can all prevent a great deal of trouble, in any situation, by listening intentionally to what someone else tries silently to scream.

✳✳✳

TWENTY-FOUR

SPEAK UP

"The most common way people give up their power is by thinking they don't have any."

—*Alice Walker*

---

ocus, focus, I would think, staring at the sink in my grandparents' old, dimly lit country house. Focusing my mind on something else kept me from realizing what was happening while I was being molested. If I opened my mouth, told an adult, would anyone believe me, or would I be kicked to the curb? Fear and desperation to survive can stifle your voice at any age. In time, I learned a person doesn't just need to speak up; they need to develop a voice for *how* they speak: "What do I truly need to say and why?"

My answer to that is simple. Speak for yourself first, and then speak for those who can't. We shouldn't have to scream our truths into the abyss to get a point across. It starts with talking. It starts with creating a dialogue around the topic, and in my case, centering on families or caregivers with special needs loved ones. "I hear you. We hear you."

This could be a universal maxim for anyone, caregiver or not: We are never given more than we can take. We are never given more than what our unique character traits and personalities can handle. As a survivor, a child who thought of her baby sister first, and later Joshua's parent, I firmly believe we are placed in situations for a reason. Although it's natural to question *why me?* I try to address a bigger question: *Why not me? Why not me to experience this and grow?*

Hearing about my father's death, some have asked me, "Do you wish you had grown up with your dad?"

Of course, a part of me wishes that. I now ask, "Would I be the same person if the abuse and neglect had not happened to me? Would I be as strong, perseverant, and resilient as I am now?" If I had the chance to do it again, I would not be who I am.

I remember sitting down at all those MHMR (formerly known as Mental Health and Mental Retardation) offices and hospitals while diagnoses were shot off like guns: "Joshua has X, Y, and Z."

Various medical professionals told me things I already knew as a nurse: "Well, he's one of the most impulsive kids I've ever seen and you're going to have problems with ABCDE…" and the list went on.

I already knew that. The real quandary was "How can you help me with it? I know there's no fix, and I don't need a description. I need to know *how* to care for Joshua."

His therapist would say, "Here are the signs he's presenting, and this could lead to…" Although she's a wonderful, sharp professional, she couldn't tell me what was necessarily good or bad. Often with a special needs child, the ground is neutral, grey, full of "maybes" and "what-ifs." I needed to know the harder truths: Because of his sexual trauma, would he be high risk to become a pedophile or a sex criminal?

Although Joshua would never try to hurt anyone, I knew he had risk factors, and I wanted to do whatever I could to protect him or to protect others from him if need be.

To contemplate worst-case scenarios is one of the most difficult things for a parent to do. Having to acknowledge that it could even happen was bad enough, but dealing with it on a daily basis was incredibly wearing. I appreciated the therapist being bluntly honest so I wouldn't ignore possible future situations. Again, it's important to speak up. Voice anything, even if it makes you squirm, feel guilty, or second-guess yourself.

Research, learn, but don't expect to fix or master your situation. I lived under the constant weight as a pediatric nurse: "Shouldn't I know?

Shouldn't I know the answers?" Once we learn, study, and acquire a new skill, there's always more to know and always room to grow. My education and experience helped me to be successful where I am now. A nursing career, marriage, motherhood—all of those were a constant opportunity for mistakes and growth. It's okay to say to yourself you're not perfect as a caregiver. You can learn, but never expect to be top-notch in every area of life.

In the hospital, if a nurse wanted to take her maternity leave early, the team came together to assess what and how much we could take on. It was a team effort to make sure nothing was out of place. A team effort is important in anything, personal or professional. Don't avoid help. When it comes to raising a child who needs extra help, you need extra help, too. Find a team and delegate tasks. It's okay to receive more childcare or hire a nanny to get out from under the umbrella of guilt in your decision-making. I'm not saying I always made either right or wrong decisions when it came to raising Joshua, but at least I made decisions.

The three of us—Joshua, Eric, and I—needed a team. It's okay to say, "I can't do this alone."

Be cautious about the information you accept. You need discernment. Don't limit yourself to just one person or resource. If I had listened to one particular MHMR office, I would have left Joshua on the street so he would have more government resources. Sadly, that's where a lot of special needs kids end up. The rationale is that if a child is abandoned, they are triaged as needing care urgently versus a child who is deemed in a "safe environment." (More information on this topic can be found at talkpoverty.org and ncsl.org—National Conference of State Legislatures). Just because a child has stability in a secure home and within a safe environment doesn't mean they're cleared for needing fewer mental health resources. Try to find as many resources as you can as your child develops and get second opinions.

If something doesn't sound right and doesn't feel right to you, don't think that's your only option. Keep combing for opportunities that will help your child, you, and your spouse, and help you make decisions as a family and individually. I can state this example again: not having another child was actually advantageous for us, because it could have put another child at risk. It would be easy to scream out *Why?* because of my feelings, but then realizing it doesn't feel right for our situation, I turned it around from "Why should we not have another child?" to "Why not give Joshua all of our attention?"

"I love you." I said it every morning and every night. "I love you." I said it during good days and bad days.

Press as much love as you can into your loved one. Don't enable wrong behaviors, but express that they are loved. As I've told Joshua, "I love you. I have grown and learned so much from raising you, and I'm a better person because of it regardless of days like this."

Once, after he'd gotten into trouble at school, I sat him down at the table with a snack and asked, "What happened?"

Lips pursed, eyes narrowed as if he was recalling a buried feeling, all Joshua could say was his truth: "Well, mom, there's an angel on my shoulder and she's whispering for me to do good things, but there's a devil on my shoulder too, who is just screaming and screaming at me."

He further explained that he can no longer hear the angel with the devil screaming at him—so he listens to the devil to make it stop. How do you explain to a child such as Joshua that there will be times in their lives when they find themselves in these situations? How do you explain that regardless of how loudly they hear the "devil" they should do the right thing? Even cognitively-sound adults have a difficult time with this moral concept. So how can I expect Joshua to understand and make the right choice every time? We mustn't justify his words or actions based on the devil screaming in his ear.

Life is a series of choices and decisions for all of us. We all make mistakes. Typically, we take accountability and then move forward. But Joshua's mind doesn't work that way. He doesn't understand account-ability, consequences, or how to move forward. Sometimes he gets stuck in the past and it inhibits him from being in the present. I want to help him live more in the present. It's difficult not to allow my feelings of empathy for what he's been through to get in the way of teaching him accountability and consequences.

Joshua cannot read this book, but he may ask someone to read it to him. His language will always be that of listening to or recounting a tale. Sometimes I open my phone to little voice-activated text messages, and I begin to tear up hearing the little boy in his grown man's "written voice"—someone yearning to be acknowledged and accepted. I know he's not texting or writing that message, but he's saying it. People like Joshua are trying to speak. They're trying to communicate, and it's our job to listen.

We would do well to tell their story, so they don't have to scream it.

❊❊❊

TWENTY-FIVE

EPILOGUE

"**M**om," he stamped his words down. "The lease is going to be up, and I need to make some decisions."

"Yes, Joshua," I answered. "What do you think about moving back with us?"

Although Eric and I had spent time speaking about next steps and knew the best option would be for him to move back with us so we could help him get back on track, I wanted him to feel like he had a choice and a voice in the decision.

I had become increasingly concerned about Joshua's mental health and state of mind during the years of the pandemic. He had become even more isolated and was finding unhealthy ways to cope.

"I feel so alone these days," he said to me during one of our phone calls. Like many people stuck at home, Joshua turned to video games and social media to grasp at any connection with the world around him. As he became more and more desperate to make connections and take control, his social media posts became more inappropriate–cursing, smoking, and dark thoughts. During this time, he had also stopped taking his medications and believed "Big Pharma" was trying to take control of his life. I knew the isolation was causing him to become more paranoid.

A day or two after asking Joshua what he thought about moving back with us, I received a message from him. He had become very good with his Scribe app so even though his words would not transcribe correctly I knew what he was saying.

"Mom, I thought about it, and I think the best place for me is by your side." I cherished messages like this from him because it gave me hope that deep within his troubled mind, he was still the little boy I loved so much.

I had done thorough research on the resources that might be available to him and believed he would have a better opportunity of finding his identity and independence closer to us. I spoke to Joshua about his expectations and how Eric and I would try to give him every opportunity to find a job, find a place to live and to help him get a dog. Having a dog was important to him. He has always had a desire to have and care for something that depended on him. I believe it was a way for him to prove his importance in the world.

During one of our phone calls, he asked, "Mom, do you still live in Texas?" Although I had mentioned our move to Arizona on multiple occasions, he didn't hear it. With adult children on the spectrum or with special needs, one must understand they might come off as a bit solipsistic. They are still living in their own world day-to-day and may not grasp details of another person's life. Some would write this off as selfish, but special needs individuals are hyper-fixated on their own world, survival, and needs.

In July of 2022, as his lease came to an end, I flew to Pennsylvania to pack him up and move him to Arizona. It has not been an easy road for any of us. After many years of Eric and I being alone, we had become accustomed to doing what we wanted when we wanted. We had no idea whether we could even go out to dinner and allow Joshua to be home alone with the dogs. But we discovered that because of his desire to take care of someone or something, he thrived on having the responsibility to feed the dogs and spend time with them.

Because Joshua had not been taking any medications, we found him to be severely dysregulated. One moment he was fine and the next he would be raging. At one point, after I asked him not to carry a knife around the house or out in the community, he became so enraged he threatened to call the police on me for violating his rights. We had many of these types of situations. Our priority was to find him a doctor who could evaluate and start him on mood stabilizers.

In almost every conversation we would remind Joshua of lessons we tried to instill in him over the years. We shared that all those things would be important for him as he ventured out on his own: people skills, the financial acumen to maintain a household, and taking care of himself. I admit, it is frustrating to say for the hundredth time, "Take a shower, brush your teeth, clean your room."

Recently during one of these conversations I asked Joshua, "What have you learned from us, do you not remember anything?" His frustration grew and he walked away in silence. Late that night he sent me this message: "Honest, true mom, the only thing I've learned from you and Eric is you are perfect for one another. You love in a way that I want to love a woman. Grandma and Grandpa were the same too. You asked me what I learned from you today and the truth is I learned that being in love with somebody is what I want. I've learned I am proud to call you and Eric my mom and dad. Even if I didn't come from your womb, in my heart and body and soul, I know you are my parents. I have nothing without you. I want to find someone to love like you found dad." I could barely get through the tears to read his text to Eric. If there had only been one thing I would want him to learn, it would be LOVE.

It has taken almost an entire year to get him established with the state resources, a physician, and somewhat of a routine. We all continue to struggle, as it has not been easy for Joshua to hold down a job or be financially stable enough to get a place of his own. We try to remain optimistic that that day will come.

That's what we all need to grant ourselves: a day to look forward to. We can all live for today, for the present, but giving yourself or your special needs loved one a goal which pushes you both away from stagnancy is important. You don't have to sit in place, wait for outsider acceptance and validation or help, or scream inside, "Things aren't changing." Life will change either way.

Eric, Joshua, and I cherish the moments we can come together for a meal or a movie or just sit in silence, appreciating what we have experienced—what we have lived through and what we have learned from each other. We have kept our goals for Joshua intact: that he would not harm himself, he would not harm anyone else, and that we would always be there for him. That Joshua would be secure in his identity, have choice, and have a voice.

❈❈❈

ACKNOWLEDGMENTS

To my husband Eric: you're the one who experienced this story in the flesh. You saw it with your own eyes and stuck with me on the journey. Our love really knows no bounds in that, and I'm grateful for all our memories—the good, bad, and ugly—and the memories yet to come. You complete my life and whether you see it or believe it, you complete Joshua's life. Forever and two days after, my love.

Joshua, you are my greatest teacher in this life. I have learned to truly laugh, cry, feel, and discover through your striving, colorful spirit. You are irreplaceable, one in a billion, yet you speak through all of us. I love you, Boober!

Allison, you have been a constant stabilizer even through the unstable times. I have leaned on you more than a big sister should. I cannot thank you enough for always being there for me and supporting my desire to give Joshua a better life. You are wise beyond your years.

Dr. Alvarez, if our family had a third party to know all of us inside and out, you come to mind first. Thank you for the years of guidance, assistance, wisdom, truth, and helping us to see all the angles. Any family in our situation would be lucky to have you at their right hand. We appreciate the insight we could not have received from any other resource. You helped us believe in the possibilities but also stamped down the reality we needed to grasp.

Last but certainly not least, we couldn't have done this without the ongoing support of our family and friends. Thank you for laughing and crying with us over the years. Thank you for listening to all the Joshua stories. Thank you for listening! We love you all!

ABOUT THE AUTHOR

Rhonda has spent her life caring for others, personally and professionally. After growing up in a small northwest Pennsylvania town she made caring for others a career. As a nurse, a court-appointed child advocate, and a special needs parent advocate, she has spent the last three decades advocating for those who cannot speak for themselves.

Rhonda Thompson, DNP, MBA, RN, NEA-BC, received her nursing degree from University of Pittsburgh at Bradford. She has two master's degrees, MSN and MBA from University of Phoenix, and her Doctoral of Nursing Practice from Rush University.

Rhonda and her husband Eric moved to Phoenix, Arizona a year ago after twenty-five years of living in Texas. They have two rescued Jack Russell terriers, Cassie and Sheldon.

CONNECT WITH RHONDA

Facebook
Facebook.com/RhondaTheSilentScreaming

LinkedIn
LinkedIn.com/in/RhondaAThompson

Interviews, Questions, or Bulk Book Orders
Rhonda.TheSilentScreaming@gmail.com

Additional Resources
TheSilentScreaming.com

THANK YOU!

Thank you for your purchase and for reading *The Silent Screaming*. This is my first book and is "indie" published so your support means the world to me. I hope you were able to connect to my story and will share with others it may help.

It would mean a lot to me if you would take a moment to write a review on Amazon so it may help others find the book.

Thank you,
Rhonda

www.ingramcontent.com/pod-product-compliance
Lightning Source LLC
Chambersburg PA
CBHW061145040426
42445CB00013B/1557